bc

COUNSELING
THE SERVICEMAN
AND HIS FAMILY

SUCCESSFUL PASTORAL COUNSELING SERIES

VOLUMES PUBLISHED OR IN PRODUCTION

Principles and Practices of Pastoral Care, by Dr. Russell L. Dicks

Ministering to the Physically Sick, by Dr. Carl J. Scherzer

Helping the Alcoholic and His Family, by Dr. Thomas J. Shipp

Marital Counseling, by Dr. R. Lofton Hudson

Counseling the Childless Couple, by The Reverend William T. Bassett

Premarital Guidance, by Dr. Russell L. Dicks

Ministering to the Dying, by Dr. Carl J. Scherzer

Ministering to Deeply Troubled People, by Dr. Ernest E. Bruder

Theology and Pastoral Counseling, by Dr. Edward E. Thornton

Group Counseling, by Dr. Joseph W. Knowles

Ministering to the Grief Sufferer, by Dr. C. Charles Bachmann

Counseling with Senior Citizens, by The Reverend J. Paul Brown

Counseling the Serviceman and His Family, by Chaplain Thomas A. Harris

Counseling the Unwed Mother, by The Reverend Helen E. Terkelsen

Counseling with College Students, by Dr. Charles F. Kemp

Preaching and Pastoral Care, by Dr. Arthur L. Teikmanis

Helping Youth in Conflict, by The Reverend Francis I. Frellick

Understanding and Helping the Narcotic Addict, by Tommie L. Duncan

Psychiatry and Pastoral Care, by Edgar Draper, M.D.

Counseling with Teen-Agers, by The Reverend Robert A. Blees and First Community Church Staff

Family Pastoral Care, Dr. Russell J. Becker

Depth Perspectives in Pastoral Work, Chaplain Thomas W. Klink

Ministering to Prisoners and Their Families, Dr. Henry H. Cassler

Referral in Pastoral Counseling, Dr. William B. Oglesby, Jr.

COUNSELING
THE SERVICEMAN
AND HIS FAMILY

THOMAS A. HARRIS

PRENTICE-HALL, INC., ENGLEWOOD CLIFFS, N.J.

Counseling the Serviceman and His Family, by Thomas A. Harris

© 1964 by Prentice-Hall, Inc., Englewood Cliffs, New Jersey.

Library of Congress Catalog Card Number: 64–20749

Printed in the United States of America.
T 18324

PRENTICE-HALL INTERNATIONAL, INC., *London*
PRENTICE-HALL OF AUSTRALIA, PTY., LTD., *Sydney*
PRENTICE-HALL OF CANADA, LTD., *Toronto*
PRENTICE-HALL OF INDIA (PRIVATE) LTD., *New Delhi*
PRENTICE-HALL OF JAPAN, INC., *Tokyo*

Third printing .... August, 1967

To my wife, whose willingness to share her husband with a demanding profession made it possible for me to put these words together, this book is lovingly dedicated.

INTRODUCTION

This series of books represents the most comprehensive publishing effort ever made in the field of pastoral care. These books could not have been published twenty-five years ago or probably even ten, for the material was not then available. In the past, single books have been available covering different phases of the task. Now we are bringing the subjects together in a single series. Here we present a library of pastoral care covering the major topics and problems that most pastors will encounter in their ministry. Fortunately, not all of these problems need be faced every week or even every month. But, when they are, the minister wants help and he wants it immediately.

These books are prepared for the nonspecialized minister serving the local church, where he is the most accessible professional person in the community. It is a well-accepted fact that more people turn to clergy when in trouble than to all other professional people. Therefore, the pastor must not fail them.

Russell L. Dicks
General Editor

CONTENTS

Introduction 7
Foreword 11

1. "What's the Difference, Anyway?"
   (*The Military Chaplain and the Civilian Pastor*) . . . 15
2. "But He Wasn't Like This at Home"
   (*Stresses of the Military Environment*) 25
3. "If We Could Only Get Together"
   (*How Separation Aggravates Problems*) 36
4. "Mrs. Jones Asked Me to Help"
   (*Co-operating Through Correspondence*) 48
5. "I Have News for You"
   (*Grief Work with the Serviceman and His Family*) . . 59
6. "He's a Good Man . . . When He's Sober"
   (*Alcohol and the Serviceman*) 71
7. "If I Could Only Get Promoted!"
   (*Financial Problems and the Military*) 83
8. "I Didn't Know It Would Be Like This"
   (*Preparing Youth for Military Life*) 96
9. "Your Church Misses You"
   (*The Home Church Follows Her Own*) 108
10. "But, Pastor, He's So Restless"
    (*Readjustment to Civilian Life*) 120
11. A Final Word
    (*Summary and Conclusion*) 133

Bibliography 137
Index 139

Contents

FOREWORD

The seeds of the ideas for this book were sown in the mind of Chaplain (Lt. Col.) Thomas A. Harris from several sources: a strong Methodist mother; the city and church in Texas where he grew up; and the United States Army in which he served as a line officer in a hot war and a chaplain in the Cold War years. His years in seminary and further graduate study certainly crystallized and matured his professional adroitness, but the acute mind and sensitive soul were built into this Soldier of God under less formal training.

Chaplain Harris has presented various chapters of this book in give-and-take dialogue with civilian clergymen and Army chaplains. This brisk dialogue was carried out at the Officers' Clubs on many posts, in the faculty lounge and on the platform of the U.S. Army Chaplain School, in the formal atmosphere of the civilian Monday morning ministerial meetings, and in the hearty atmosphere of the Army mess halls and kitchens of many Army quarters. The spontaneousness of its written form is testimony to the sparkling mind, sharp pen, and warm heart of the author.

This book has been needed for many years—it cuts deep, but the pen is skillful and sure and the heart of the author is right. As an old Army man, I am proud to offer these humble words of encouragement to the reader. If the pen seems sharp even in print and the words are soul-searing at times, Chaplain Harris wrote them for the use of men of flesh and blood seeking a better way of serving Almighty God and his needy children.

Take courage, "We are not treated as whited sepulchers full of dead men's bones"; indeed, we are encouraged by the author as the Lord's practitioners of faith, hope, and charity. Chaplain Harris simply dresses our parishioners up in military uniform and sets them down in our offices with muddy boots, sweaty clothes, clenched teeth, and tear-filled eyes, then stands beside us as we organize our first steps on the way of helping this military man and his family.

I am proud to be a small part of this warm, courageous approach to so passion-filled an area of human experience.

Charles E. Brown, Jr.
Chaplain (Major General), U.S.A.
Chief of Chaplains

COUNSELING
THE SERVICEMAN
AND HIS FAMILY

CHAPTER ONE

"WHAT'S The DIFFERENCE, ANYWAY?"
(The Military Chaplain and the Civilian Pastor)

"But why take up the time of an ordained man by sending him to Chaplain School to study what he has already had?" The young, newly appointed chaplain spoke with marked intensity. He went on: "I can see why it is necessary to learn about the military way of life, the wearing of the uniform, the customs of the service, but why a course in counseling?" He paused. Receiving no answer, he added, "What's the difference, anyway, between counseling the serviceman and counseling anyone?"

Likenesses

Certainly there are many similarities in the requirements of pastoral care the world over. Basic human needs are similar enough for the professionally concerned to exchange ideas profitably. The problems of the military individual differ little from those of the civilian in the same age group.

Likenesses in the "Troubled." Both the serviceman and his family tend to live in an American enclave in all of the countries where our forces are stationed. Exotic eastern lands may sound strangely mysterious to the American stay-at-home civilian, but the military wife tends to let herself be cut off from the new and different by settling down to the "internal triangle" of home, post exchange, and commissary. The serviceman himself spends the work day with his unit. He relaxes in a service club reminding him of home, he engages in sports and plays games with other Americans, and goes to American movies on the post in his spare time. If he breaks out of the monotony of social life provided on the post, he is likely to strive to find something outside the post that is similar to what he knows at home. He frequents night clubs, bars, and theaters—all catering to

15

Americans. An unfriendly attitude on the part of the natives of the area tends to drive him deeper into post activities that simulate an American environment. Thus, many of his problems are not so different from those of his friends in the States.

People are people—and that is just the problem. American youth, wherever it is, faces the same sort of authority difficulties in struggling toward independence. Problems arising from the need to find a value system with which one can live are just as distressing the world over. The pangs of jealousy and doubt are equally intense, whether one is at home or abroad. The drive of the appetites is equally incessant in either setting. The pangs of remorse and the torture of guilt feelings are quickly spotted, whoever experiences them. Marriages are marriages the world over, and the saying is true: "There are more people married in this world than are doing well at it."

Grief strikes to the core of being as ruthlessly in civilian life as in the military. The confusion of our times expresses itself in many heartbreaking ways everywhere. Man's tendency to career up and down life's emotional roller coaster remains unchanged. The man who zooms from elation to depression and back again in civilian life will ride the same course in the military. Those who connive to evade the minimal responsibilities of the military are little different from the hometown youth who wanders through aimless day after aimless day. A chaplain just beginning his military career went immediately to the defense of each young enlisted man who came for help. After some embarrassing moments with his commander, during which his "facts" turned out not to be facts at all, he sought out a chaplain friend with more experience, who advised him: "In your mind's eye put that kid back in civilian clothes and on the street corner in front of the drugstore. Think of him as the son of an older parishioner, or as the husband of one of the girls in your church, and then think how you would feel about his present conduct." Following that advice, with necessary adjustment for each different situation, has been most productive.

The theologically tinged questions man asks of life are the same wherever you find him. The man struggling with feelings and thoughts about God carries the same fight with him despite mobility or locale. The person whose guilt feelings drive him to come to terms with Almighty God is seen everywhere. The individual whose aimlessness and lack of meaning make it all the more urgent for him to make sense of the universe seeks out military chaplain and civilian clergyman alike, depending on which is available. The human being longing for an assurance of life eternal is the same person, no matter where you find him.

The same unceasing battleground of emotional conflict exists for the serviceman as it does for the civilian. His problems neither vanish nor change greatly by virtue of his enlistment. Despite the sacrificial demands of some military assignments, the noteworthy fact is that individuals seem to experience somewhat the same problems wherever they light. A man who grew up in emotional combat with a rigid father will recall in the counseling session how he was mistreated in school, on his civilian job, and how he is used unjustly by his present commander. Most of us spend our lives seeking a new setting for the same problems. Our inward battles find new battlefields. We can always find "objective" excuses for our "selfless" struggle against injustice. The man with many divorces finds that each woman he marries is unworthy of his trust. The woman who has trouble as an American housewife will have the same trouble when she joins her husband in Germany, Africa, Japan, or Okinawa.

Likenesses in the "Helpers." The so-called "helping" persons, wherever they are, like the troubled ones they strive to help, have a similar pattern. The "helper's" motivation, insights, and ability to function effectively are fairly constant despite title, position, and location.

The web of motivation is too intricate to unravel fully. While working with its various strands, we must not fall into the trap of reductionism. We must not say, as some do, that because the sadist *enjoys* inflicting pain on others and the surgeon *has to* inflict pain on his patients, the two are the same. We ought not to equate the paranoid and the policeman because both live under the domination of suspicion and doubt. It may be true that the clergyman, who is striving to come to terms with God the Father, is often closely related to his brother, who is still threatened by his earthly father, but it is not fair to say the two are the same in every respect. Yet it can be helpful to scrutinize our motivation carefully, if we do not oversimplify the matter. Perhaps most people who function well in a helping role do so because of their need to work on their own problems. Yet, the counselor's own problems do not necessarily disqualify him from helping others. Indeed, the capacity to understand the emotional struggles of others is increased when one has fought similar battles. Apparently then, the emotions that attracted us into a helping role are similar, whether we serve in the pastorate or in the chaplaincy. The chaplain and the pastor work in the context of the same difficulties. If one operates as an ecclesiastical errand boy, he will do so in the civilian community or on the military post. If he is an advice giver, he will dispense his bromides in or out of uniform. If he prescribes theological answers for the cure of souls, he will continue to minister in this authoritarian way. The chaplain who told me: "I like to have people come to me in trouble because it gives me a chance to explain my theology" had, I am sure, said the same thing in civilian life.

The chaplain whose primary identification is with his mother will identify most of the premarital and marital problems he encounters as the result of the callousness of men. He will write tearful letters of sympathy and condolence to wives whose husbands don't trust them. This he would do whether he wore a "dog collar" or "dog tags." On the other hand, the man whose "maleness" is threatened by "feminine" urges will identify himself with the strong and noble soldier who is let down by a weak wife or girl friend.

The naturally talkative "helper" will say, "What these people need is for someone to *tell* them when they are wrong and to *tell* them what they must do about it. If I don't tell them, who will?" He will say, "I am trained to understand these problems and I would be letting my people down if I didn't tell them . . . discussion is irrelevant in matters of morality." This he will do whatever his locale. By the same token, the passive individual, fearful of rejection, looking at life as a continual popularity contest that he is doomed to lose, will recoil from any pressures on him to express his own views to one in trouble. He will learnedly uphold "nondirective" counseling over "directive," not realizing the uselessness of such labels.

The clergyman whose attitudes are dominated by the fear of death tends to concentrate on assisting the bereaved. Often he will become a chaplain, hospital or military or both, but wherever he serves, his own problems will determine the type of problem to which he responds most deeply. The man with authority problems tends to work most readily with others possessed of the same attitudes. The clergyman confused by the swirling turmoil of inner drives strives to explain away problems in others. As he is successful, he feels better within

himself. The problems of others are in some measure our own problems "writ large." This is true whether we are at home or in the
service.

Differences

Certain differences must be understood before the pastor can
minister helpfully to the serviceman or his family. Whether they are
differences in kind or in degree, they are deviations that ought to be
recognized. The hometown pastor working with the serviceman's
family should strive to recognize the problems of the chaplain, as
well as those of the serviceman.

Differences in the "Troubled." It takes a long time for the
military to replace the feeling of security the individual has associated with his home for so long. This cannot be done for those who
serve only a short time. Many serve their "hitch" without ever learn-
ing to trust the military environment. The lack of feelings of security
based on the familiar intensifies ordinary problems.

A short-termer in the military runs into the same sort of emotional problems that he could have handled at home, but due to the
strangeness of his environment he may need help. The matter is
made worse by the fact that he often does not know where to turn.
Feeling both friendless and helpless, he may tend to become more
dependent on the chaplain. He may cling frantically to the first offer
of help. He talks to the chaplain, and the chaplain listens like a good
father. He can relax and talk without worrying about his words being
used against him. He can forget about military jargon and pour out
his problems. The chaplain is the Church to him. Even if the serviceman was not much of a churchman at home, he probably knows the
role of the Church in the community. Any representative of that
Church becomes a bridge to life back home. One danger here is that
he may be only too willing to put aside his own responsibility for his
life and depend too heavily on any "advice" he receives. If the chaplain he meets likes to give advice, any relief the serviceman finds may
be only symptomatic. Such help may make it harder for him to
handle similar problems later. Thus, one difference between the
troubled person in the military and the same man at home (if he
could be in both places at once) is a tendency toward an inappropri-
ate childlike dependency when problems loom large.

Another difference is related to the predominant role of authority difficulties in the service. A civilian who has problems stemming from his feelings toward authority has enough trouble. He has teachers in school, professors in college, employers, doctors, policemen, lawyers, and others—but he does not have to live with them! In the service he has military policemen, military physicians, military lawyers, and others—and he also has the total structure of command from which he cannot escape, day or night. Everywhere he turns he sees authority. Some, who are immediately over him, live in the same barracks. At work he is surrounded by those in authority. One of his main tasks is to learn to obey his superiors instinctively. This he must learn if he is to be useful to his unit in combat. If he does not respond quickly to the voice of command in some situations, he may lose his life. He may also forfeit the lives of others who depend on him. Today military men are taught more and more to act on their own initiative while carrying out orders, but basic orders must nonetheless be obeyed. It is not that such a relationship to authority is in itself destructive, but rather that the serviceman with authority problems lives in constant emotional tension. He is like an alcoholic forced to earn his living by working in a cocktail lounge. He cannot escape the threat of his problem.

Even if he goes to the chaplain for help his problem reappears, for the chaplain has the trappings of authority. In the classroom sessions, which are a mandatory part of the character guidance program in the Army, I have always striven toward freedom of expression. I used to be puzzled by how hard it was to get the soldier to bare his thoughts. Finally it flashed through my mind that when I stood before the soldier with my Crosses and my insignia of rank it was hard for him to share his thoughts openly because he was suddenly confronted by two huge institutions. To him, I represented both Church and military establishment, a pretty hard pill for anyone to take easily. Both institutions stir up dark feelings, as well as helpful emotions, in most people. The military chaplain ought to recognize this fact and learn to accept its twofold role, while at the same time minimizing its threatening overtones when he is face-to-face with his people.

The serviceman's problems are further complicated by the simple fact that he is cut off from loved ones at home. Normally insignificant problems become more threatening. Run-of-the-mill problems that beset the household can, when he is at home, often be settled quietly and satisfactorily. The same simple problem subjected to the long, deadly delay of even the most efficient modern postal service can grow to major proportions. Besides, few Americans can express themselves clearly and adequately through correspondence. To write a letter explaining uncomplicated courses of desired actions is simply beyond some of us. By the time answers come, the questions have changed. They have already had an answer enforced by the tyranny of time. If the improvised answer is not in accord with the wishes of the absent member, trouble arises. Problems related to the training, health, or general welfare of children, or financial matters can breed disagreements when one of the parents is far from home. The breakdown in communications is often the villain of the piece. It is hard enough to communicate ideas even when living under the same roof. The military situation intensifies such problems. This needs to be considered by the chaplain overseas, the pastor at home, and the people in trouble.

It is simply true that ordinary human problems are complicated by any break in the oneness of home life. The fact that the military chaplain spends much of his time with those facing marital problems is no reflection on the military home. Many marriages are poorly conceived in the first place. Many spouses continue the marital relationship only because societal sanctions make it difficult to do otherwise. Neighborhood couples ride out the same storms of marital discord. Furthermore, the opportunities for succumbing to temptation are fewer. But, transport one of the spouses away from the other and away from old Mrs. Grundy next door, and you have the working formula for marital breakdown. The people involved are not one whit better or worse than those who do not face the destructive possibility posed by miles of separation. The military family must face the added threat of months of separation leading to misunderstanding, lack of trust, and the real problem of the ready availability of those of the opposite sex all too willing to "understand." The fact that it takes a strongly united family to meet and overcome such obstacles is a testimonial to the worth of so many of our military families.

Servicemen experience repeated periods of enforced loneliness. The deep craving for another who seems to care is like the deep, gnawing pain of a physical disorder. One who is ordinarily in command of his thoughts may find his emotional fortress stormed and overthrown. The gloomy darkness that enshrouds the mind when one feels isolated from those of like mind will pervade a man's life. The light of hope may flicker and die down. The misery of "aloneness" is a recurrent problem to the serviceman. Such a pervading note of near-despair will certainly add to the complexity of any problem that comes along. The pastor at home needs to know what such moments can produce in letters written while under the spell. He needs to know the danger of agreeing to courses of action decided upon while one of the spouses is living in a miasma of loneliness. Surely such feelings are universal enough to arouse answering feelings in the heart of the "helper."

Another problem built into the military life is that resulting from the fear of releasing aggressive impulses even when socially permitted and professionally required to do so. In our American "good Joe" culture, which even in the midst of a highly competitive business world stresses getting along with others, military men must learn to express aggression directly. This is not easy for most. An individual with such a problem in civilian life will be in trouble in the service. Related to this problem is that of being forced to recognize the potential destructiveness of modern war. In civilian life it is easier to delude oneself through ceaseless activity or selective blindness as to the threat of universal holocaust. The military person must accept the threat, for his job is to hold back such a possibility. The military is a protective arm of the civilian community, spawned by "the great republic." It must do the dirty linen of the body politic. The civilian can more easily deny his part in such a bloody potential. The serviceman has this emotional burden added to those burdens which are common to us all.

Differences in the "Helpers." As the troubled person in the military has certain problems accentuated by the nature of his life, so does the military chaplain. He shares the problems of his people. His problems include those of authority, separation, loneliness, and the basic problem of war itself. As a man of God, he has even more extreme problems in accepting the destructive potential of his group. He can easily be thrown off the track by a counselee asking, "Chaplain, how can you, as a man of God, serve an organization dedicated to war?" or a similar question. If the chaplain is not alert to the nature of the threat, he may often launch forth into sermonizing about war and peace and the nature of God. Actually, back of the question may be only the fact that the soldier had been denied a three-day pass.

The chaplain must work through his own conflicts and the problems of his role if he is to do his work well. How he works the problem out will depend largely upon his nature and the theological system to which he is committed. A standard answer for this problem is not possible. Each chaplain must strive to understand his own emotions about his work, or they will sell him short at one time or another. The civilian pastor has trouble enough in coming to terms with his society, but such trouble is not accentuated by the need to face the destructive potential of his culture every hour of every day.

Loneliness is just as gripping and real for the chaplain overseas as it is for the serviceman he hopes to help. A certain amount of identification with his people is helpful, but to be reduced to a whimpering heap along with the troubled counselee serves only to compound the problem. Loneliness may gnaw at the insides of the chaplain, crying out to be deadened by alcohol or sexual involvement. To follow such a course is to damage the chaplain's usefulness as a moral influence in the military community. Simply overcoming such temptations overtly is not enough. The chaplain must remember that in his primal being these appetites and drives and fears are constantly awaiting an opportunity to express themselves—if not directly, then vicariously. Thus, the military chaplain should ask himself some soul-searching questions when his counseling takes on primarily sexual overtones. When all problems that he deals with are seen as sexual in nature and he finds himself spending more time on lascivious details, the danger signals are up! He must not give the idea that he approves moral laxity, nor must he let himself become rejecting and destructive in his reactions. Military chaplains handle such challenges well. Yet, the challenges are real and are best handled out in the open by professional discussion. Such matters cannot be swept under the rug.

If the civilian pastor is to understand the problems that beset the chaplain in his work, he ought also to recognize the strangely compelling power of authority problems in the lives of most clergymen. He can then see something of what the chaplain has to face. So many clergymen are drawn toward the ministry in the first place by the need to become one with "father." The chaplain may have the same problem doubled in spades. The military environment is a perfect lure for people with such problems. The answer in resolving aggressive feelings against "father" seems to lie in getting so close to him that you are almost one. Such a tendency would certainly color most counseling.

The clergyman, civilian or military, working with servicemen and their families must make sure that the drive to be one with "father" stays out of the way as he struggles to help. If he does not, he will often bog down in counseling with a spirited defense of the military. Such a defense is understood by the counselee for what it is, a basic lack of trust in the very entity one attempts to support. A better defense is to be able to accept attacks on the system quietly and without a spoken defense. When such supercharged feelings are released in an atmosphere of calm acceptance, the counselee often finds it easier to come to terms with the basic problem. That problem may be something quite different. Such problems are rarely the abstractions first encountered in the interview. More likely they center on a disturbing letter from home or difficulty with someone in the unit. The chaplain and the pastor will have a hard time isolating the real problems if their own authority problems take precedence over those of the people who come for help. Alert and fairly well-balanced clergymen can detect such feelings in themselves and rob them of their destructive effect. This is a problem common to all who seek to minister to the needs of others, but it tends to be intensified in the life of the chaplain.

Conclusion

People are pretty much the same the world over. Their problems are recognizable wherever they are seen. It would be ridiculous for the clergyman to be blind to this fact. However, similarities can be harmful if their very familiarity blinds us to the differences. Differences do exist in degree if not in kind. The military life emphasizes and intensifies certain problem areas. The clergyman, civilian or military, ministering to the serviceman and his family should study both likenesses and differences in the problems of his parishioners. He must also be aware of certain traps that lie in wait for him. A consideration of such matters should make us all better able to help our people.

CHAPTER TWO

"BUT HE WASN'T LIKE THIS At HOME"

(Stresses of the Military Environment)

The letter was fairly long and disorganized, but the anxiety of the writer was clear. The chaplain had received many such letters in his years with the military. Always they left a feeling of frustration. The drive to help was certainly there, but he had found the ability to cope with baffling human problems is limited at best.

In essence, the letter from a worried mother told of her concern for her son. During a period of eighteen months she had received only two or three letters from him. "He doesn't seem to care how I feel," she wrote, "and he wasn't like that at home." According to her note, while her son was at home and in school he had always been most thoughtful and considerate. He had been sensitive to her feelings and had always tried to please her. A faithful churchgoer, he had never caused any trouble. The two had been quite close. The boy's father, a steady worker and a good provider, was rather distant emotionally. The boy and his mother had been even closer because of that. When he first went overseas, after a period of service in the States, he had written every day. After a month or two, the letters became infrequent and finally he ceased writing altogether.

The last letter she had received had come after she had asked the Red Cross to check into the matter. A field director at the post had called him in for a chat. The boy was in good health and apparently in no trouble, therefore the matter was closed. The field director and the boy had both written and things seemed all right. Since then, six months had elapsed without another letter.

The Pressure of Boredom

It was now the chaplain's duty to locate the young man and strive to find out what was going on. In such cases it is necessary to approach the problem with as much understanding as possible, lest

25

the contact be futile. It is an embarrassing thing for a supposedly "adult" male to be called in by the chaplain and be confronted with a letter from home. It is even worse if there is an identification of the chaplain with the authority system. "I was ordered to see you and am complying with that order" is an attitude that makes effective work most difficult. In this case, the young man, Sergeant William F. Engles, was detailed to duty away from his company headquarters. The chaplain got through to Engles without involving any of his commanders and arranged to see him at a time convenient for both. As long as it is possible to handle a matter by only involving the person concerned, it is much easier to build a good, working relationship. Young chaplains tend to use the "system" too readily.

"I have a letter from your mother," the chaplain said, "she wanted me to look you up and see how things are going with you. It seems that everything is all right at home, but she had not heard from you for so long, that she began to wonder if you were all right."

"Yes, Chaplain, I understand. You see she does worry very easily . . . and she is quite right. I just can't make myself write home. Really I can't. My job is all right. I like it very much, but it does keep me busy at the same old thing over and over, so there really isn't much to write about. When I'm not on duty, I bowl or go to the movies, or maybe to the beach. But there isn't much to say about any of that. And when I try to write it sounds all depressed and I don't like to think over what has already happened."

"You seem to be in pretty much of a rut and it gets you down."

"Well," said Engles, "it isn't so bad, I guess. My work does keep me busy and I did make sergeant pretty fast. I've got no real gripes. I just don't have anything to write about. You know how it is, don't you?"

Perhaps I didn't know how it was, but having been faced with much the same kind of problem many times, I think I had some idea of what was going on. Actually, I could remember back to my own time in the Pacific during World War II and how difficult it was to write. "Every day," as one of the men had put it then, "was just like looking in the face of a dead horse." This was an earthy, but highly accurate setting forth of a state of mind. Apparently endless routine, even when its ultimate purpose can be seen, is extremely difficult to cope with. Much of what is necessary for the military organization is repetitive. Most needs which men have are recurrent.

Rations and clothing, for instance, have to be provided no matter what. Tasks connected with such demands are often dull. Man works at getting rid of things and cleaning up after himself all of his life. Then he dies, and someone has to get rid of him. Life can easily be viewed, in Fred Allen's phrase about a career in radio, as a "treadmill to oblivion."

Routine may be necessary but is always difficult to accept gracefully. A moment of martyrdom is easier to bear than months of massive dullness. Being bored to death is a hard way to go. In Sergeant Engles' case dullness had been fairly well accepted when he first had to face it, but he didn't want to have to face it *again* in writing about it. Aside from the discomfort caused his mother, Engles' was practically a success story. His reaction had been to turn away from others, to avoid involvement at a deeper level; he just did not talk about his feelings. In some ways his mother may have been better off. She at least did not have to read depressing letters, which might have provoked anxiety on her part. Engles knew how hard it was to sound happy when he wasn't. Even if he was not actively unhappy, if he had to concentrate on the dullness his letters might sound like the last outcry of a potential suicide. At least they might have so sounded to an anxious mother.

The overcast of monotony that accompanies so much of the military life, even in the midst of combat, has been made clear through such books as *Mr. Roberts* and others that have attempted to grasp the emotional flavor of sheer dullness. Men react in strange ways to such pressures. Engles simply refused to think about it. If something within him had died, he at least had strength of mind enough to do his job well and to carry on.

The chaplain checked with the Red Cross field director, who got out his file on Engles and reported very much the same type of conversation the chaplain had just had. After that, Engles had written, and his mother had been put at ease for a time. Then tedium again set in. True, other matters may have been at work here. Perhaps the relationship with mother through the years had been the result of her desire more than his. Perhaps she had used her son as a way of finding emotional relief when her husband seemed cold. Now in a distant land with a new life, the son had turned away from enforced dependency. Perhaps even if the young man did not recognize it, he was basically glad to be away from such closeness. Not that he did not love his mother, but other feelings arising from a need to stand alone had taken over in his life. The letters may not have been written because he didn't want to keep as close to his mother as he had earlier.

Perhaps such a state of affairs might have been drawn out in a long-term counseling relationship, but the motivation for such hard work was simply not there. It is very difficult in the military service to sustain such a relationship, due to frequent changes of assignment on the part of counselors and counselees alike. Also the demands of emergency situations calling for immediate "patch-up" jobs are so strong and so numerous that there is little time for more involved treatment. Often the "helper" is inadequately trained for such work, had he the time.

Engles left, promising to write. The chaplain wrote Mrs. Engles, stating that he had seen her son. He reported the young man to be in good health, but quite busy at a demanding, though monotonous job. He expressed understanding of her feelings and asked her to write him at any time he might be of help. He promised to try to keep in contact with the boy. Although he regretted the anxiety caused by Engles' failure to write, actually he was sure that Engles was handling his boredom better than many others at the same station.

The "Pressure" of Freedom

Often the burden of letters to the chaplain is one of fear for the absent one's moral welfare. Parents and wives read newspapers, books, and magazines. They watch television and they go to the movies. Also, they are attuned to the feelings of the absent loved one and they sense when things are going wrong. Sometimes a man from the same unit returns to the hometown and his stories reach fearful ears. "But he wasn't like that when he was at home, Chaplain, so please see him and see what you can do."

More often than not such fears are groundless. Most men make such transitions fairly adequately. They talk a tougher game than they play. They may be afraid to admit their high ideals in a bull session, but they are often much more afraid to part with built-in moral standards. Where the home training has been good and the emotional reward of past relationships has been sufficient, the American soldier produces amazing moral stability. With inadequate home training and only minimal emotional returns, then the problem becomes increasingly difficult, for the pressures are real. Actually the pressures are the result, in these cases, of "lack of pressure," in one sense. There is little pressure exerted to hold the man in line morally. There is no longer any fear of old Mrs. Fraley across the street or down the block. There is no danger that the boss will fire him because the neighbors are talking and it is hurting business. The soldier has to have his own dynamic inner ethic, if he is to be unscathed.

Not only is there little pressure to keep him in line, there is a form of pressure toward immorality. It is the pressure of the peer group. In the history of man, the military service has been a way of life for the so-called "manly." The soldier responding to the civilian image has too often felt a need to prove his virility by promiscuity, heavy drinking, and brawling. Thus he thinks he has shown himself to be a "man." The fact is that such "proofs" tend rather to establish insecurity and immaturity than "manliness." The professional soldier knows that such conceptions are misconceptions. He knows that the best soldier is the man with strength of character, on whom heavy responsibilities can be placed with the sure knowledge that he will measure up. But the young soldier is convinced otherwise. He has an image of the soldier as wild and thoughtless, and he sets out to live up to that image. He does not yet know that the military service is opposed to such nonsense; that it indeed punishes those whose failings reach command attention. He wants to be a "man," and his definition of a "man" is worse than infantile because now he has the muscle power and the physical development required to put otherwise harmless infantile drives into action.

Add the actual pressure of group standards to the lack of pressure toward morality, and you are in trouble. Press on to the fact that in many overseas assignments opportunities for the irresponsible expression of primitive drives are myriad, and the trouble is clearly apparent. In many areas where the American serves, the people have striven to discover his "weaknesses" and to cater to them. Since the American will pay for the opportunity to express his basic drives irresponsibly, the native inhabitant adapts his or her life to the accompaniment of the ring of the cash register. Whole communities spring up dedicated to the desires of the American serviceman. Alcohol and sex are the basic condiments. Violence follows quickly.

Throw into the pot the dullness and monotony which Engles met fairly successfully, but which are quite too much for others, and you have what appears to be an abrupt change in character on the part of many. The question is, is it really a change, or is it true that now the real personality of the individual is exposed for what it always was? Perhaps our vaunted morality is only a morality of fear. An inner dynamic may simply be missing from our lives. The "religious" way has simply been the way of the community. We should have been aware of this fact for many years, for the activities of the American away from his hometown for a week or a week end have been far from exemplary.

The matter of the serviceman and his conduct is even more complex. Added to the problems already mentioned is the fact of his average age. Many servicemen are at an age when, even at home, they would have to be in rebellion against the authority of parents. The young man on the way from adolescence to maturity has a difficult road in any case. He must struggle to stand alone, to find his own legs, to be the person he is. He needs to find some way to make the struggle explicit. In other times he might have dramatized his need by painting the water tower of a school in another town or by transplanting the statue of a community hero to the community toilet in the middle of town. He might have been suspended from college for a few days for a foolish exploit; he might even have been thrown out of college for his part in a student riot; he might have startled his clergyman uncle by going all out for atheism. In some communities today the problem is even more destructively expressed. The gang rumbles and the week-long beer parties on the beach are probably an expression of the problems involved in growing up.

The drive toward independence meets, in the serviceman, with the loss of familiar community values, and the addition of the standards of a new group. It may be somewhat reassuring to observe that the problem remains basically the same. However, it must be understood on the basis of the setting in which it is found—that of military life a long way from home.

The remarkable thing is the success that trained commanders and senior non-commissioned officers have in helping young men with their problems. The men who make up the nucleus of the unit recognize these problems instinctively and work to overcome them. The drive to build a high unit spirit is one answer to the destructiveness of the breakdown in morality. If young soldiers can believe in the work of the small group they serve, they can build up a bulwark against temptation. If their pride in being physically fit and mentally alert is strong, then they will return to the fold after their youthful experiments with immorality. It is not enough to warn them of the troubles they may have when they go home, or to uphold the highest values of their nation, unless, they first can believe in the group with which they live. Actually, both long-range and idealistic goals and the practical goals of the immediate group work to reinforce one another. The point is that the practical understanding of the leaders of the unit, who may know little about sociology or psychology, often accomplishes more towards strengthening the moral fibre of the individual, than all the experts in the world. Never discount the therapeutic value of a good, strong first sergeant.

Some Answers That Fail

True, the commander and his non-commissioned associates have a lot of help. In the military the number of character-building resources has proliferated. On any military post you will find service clubs, gymnasiums, bowling centers, chapel and chapel activities, and other facilities—all striving to give the serviceman a wholesome opportunity to work off some of his drives. You will find the resources of all these groups brought to bear on the problem. When the commander expresses his problems to these organizations, they are strong to cooperate. Mental hygiene clinics and their trained personnel are becoming increasingly active in the use of preventive techniques. In many instances psychiatrically trained individuals are going out to the small unit level to confer with local leadership and to recommend changes designed to assist morale and to resist the drift toward destructive habits. Some chaplains are beginning to feel that their traditional area of work is being invaded. Others are happy to welcome any sort of assistance in facing a common problem. Chaplains are redoubling their efforts to stay in contact with the problem. They are active members of the unit character-guidance council, they instruct in matters dealing with morality, ethics, and patriotism, in addition to the religious instruction which they provide on a voluntary basis. Also participating in the effort to help are military wives, whose groups (such as the Women of the Chapel) strive to offer church socials and fellowship gatherings to make the young soldier feel at home away from home. Chaplains organize their activities to fit in with the military schedule and seek out young men to usher, teach, and sing in the choirs.

But the tragic thing is that the on-post activities designed to win the man from his baser desires in many cases are fighting an unimpressive, if not a losing battle. Service clubs are often deserted or poorly attended. Gymnasiums are crowded only during basketball season, and then only while the games are actually being played. The non-commissioned officers' clubs and enlisted men's clubs draw many of their people when they are on the way somewhere else. The chapel often becomes an activity for dependent wives, their husbands, and their children, and is filled by unmarried soldiers only when unit competition is sparking attendance. Many times the single soldier says, that instead of feeling at home at the church gatherings, he is offended by the presence of the fine women who strive to help him.

And why is all of this? Of course there is no one answer. One can say that the soldier stays away from the chapel activity because it makes him homesick. This is the answer often given by the soldier: "Chaplain, I know I used to go to church at home, but it isn't the same here . . . anyway, it reminds me of home and makes me so homesick I can't stand it." This was an answer given after a soldier had described himself as a constant churchgoer at home, but one who had fallen away at this particular assignment. This answer is just too easy. It is a defensive reaction in most cases. Actually, the soldier simply does not know why he stays away.

One answer that casts some light is that people just do not like to think of other people striving to keep them in line. There is an air of patronage in such an approach. "Why do these people think they are so good that they have to help us?" No one likes to be a "thing" sought out to be saved. There is a healthy note to such rebellion. Perhaps this is part of the answer. It is hard to attend activities organized to "do good" without in a sense being aware of the smugness of those seeking to be "do-gooders." Yet it can also be observed that the condescension and the self-righteousness the soldier senses are not as extreme or extensive as he thinks. His reaction is highly overconditioned. He knows his need to be helped and he assumes others are always conscious of his needs. Actually, those so-called "do-gooders" may not be as stuffy as he thinks. They may feel themselves more closely identified to him than he is ready to believe. He cannot give them credit for sincerity, because then he may suddenly feel the need to do something about his mistakes. To let someone get close might mean to be forced to do something about his own life. So he runs and cries "Pharisee."

Why won't the men go to activities that are so like those at home? Why does the man who is a churchman at home turn away from the church in a distant land? The answers thus far advanced all cast some light. All are partially true when applied to the individual case. But there is at least one more approach. It may be that the serviceman, particularly the young serviceman in his late teens or early twenties, retreats from the Church because it does remind him of home. Not because it makes him homesick, but because he is in rebellion against the disciplines of home. At home he would be fighting the disciplines of the Church. It is no wonder he is doing so away from home.

The Church reminds him of mother and father, and he is now going through a time in his personal development that demands that he break the clutch of home. He has been necessarily dependent on his parents for so long that it is inconceivable that he can become a person until he breaks their spell. Instinctively he knows that they are inadvertently determined to keep him under the warm waters of dependency. He knows he will always be his "mama's boy" or his "father's son" unless he makes a strong stand.

At such a time it is well known that his peer group becomes his master. At home he has to dress like his gang, however sloppy its members may be, he has to be accepted by his gang—he is not going to be called "chicken." At home there is some help in the fact that he does not live with the gang. He may spend many hours with them but he does come home, and some contact is maintained, however tenuous. In the service, however, he lives in the barracks with his gang. He never escapes them.

It is known that the best means of his coming through the period of adolescence without serious scars is a good adult friend outside of the family. If a young man has a teacher he admires, a coach he responds to, or some adult he has met outside of the family circle and toward whom he can feel warmth, then his life is made. Thus it is that the leaders in his unit are often better able to help him than are the professional "helpers" such as the chaplains. He does not necessarily identify his platoon leader with his home. He may see him as a "father" figure, but not as a representative of his home. He does tend to identify the chaplain with home and mother, and it is difficult for him to overcome this.

Despite the cynical trend to downgrade the leader and to laugh at loyalty, man is still basically the same. He does respond to good leadership. He does warm up to the "just" father. He still is ready to give his life for the strong commander. He is still in search of a "hero." Often the non-commissioned leader can be of the greatest help. He lives with the men. He suffers from the commands of the leader just as they do. Whereas the company commander might be too much like father at home, the N.C.O. can be an older sibling—a big brother. The services all proclaim their need for the dedicated non-commissioned officer. They still know how invaluable he can be when he has a sense of personal responsibility for his charges.

These comments are made to point out problems involved in helping the serviceman to live a moral life; they are not intended to minimize the need for all facilities dedicated to the same end. All of the wholesome activities and facilities mentioned are valuable. Many servicemen make full use of them and are happy to have them. Nonetheless, the helping person needs to know the more sordid facts of life. If he is to avoid "patronization" and to establish real rapport, he must be aware of the pitfalls. Working together, unit commanders and their associates, chaplains, psychiatrically trained workers, and all concerned with the welfare of the serviceman and his family can accomplish much. But for the most effective work, they must both want to and know how to work together.

However the problem is analyzed, the answer is seen partially at least in a better understanding of the problems of growth and character development. If we know what the core conflict of each age is and can apply our knowledge flexibly to the individual situation, we can offer help to our people. The letter from home may say, "He wasn't like this at home," and on the surface the letter may be right, yet in a larger sense he *was* like this at home. He simply didn't have a chance to express his true nature! He is the same man and he must be approached the same way. He still needs leaders whom he can admire. He needs strong individuals who do not give in to the temptations of a less moral environment. He needs rapport with someone who is more than simply a chronological adult. He needs protection from himself. He needs an opportunity to make errors that will not forever destroy his life. He needs to prove himself and to find out for himself that some of the wisdom of his elders is truly wisdom and will remain so as long as man is man.

The counselor of the serviceman and of the serviceman's family needs to know all that he can about the man so that he can provide the understanding and the compassion necessary at critical moments of development. If he does not understand something of what is going on in the counselee, he will only be helpful by sheer chance. He can bring up his average of helpfulness by never forgetting that while individuals seem to change, those changes are ordinarily within certain recognizable limits. He can strive to provide the sort of relationship that will assist the individual within those limits. Thus, if he maintains a relationship in which he himself is strongly committed to high moral values and yet is compassionate and nonpunitive, he may provide the guidepost in the jungle of life that leads home to personal satisfaction without self-blame. If he can listen and not strike back, if he can believe in the right and understand the wrong, if he can get close enough, yet not demand dependency in return for his effort, then he can be a source of great strength to the young person struggling toward his own life.

CHAPTER THREE

"If We COULD ONLY GET TOGETHER"

(How Separation Aggravates Problems)

On the desk was a radiogram. He saw it immediately. Why is a radiogram always larger than anything else on a desk? Overreacting, he felt the overtones of tragedy. The chaplain had been away for a few days. Was there a message in the envelope that should have been handled earlier? Was it now too late? Quickly, he opened the envelope and read "No word from my son in two weeks. Please find out what is wrong." There were a return address and a slip of paper arranging for the cost of an answer. The man's name was Robert C. Karns, and he was a member of a unit which, while not that chaplain's primary responsibility, was in the area. A call to the unit orderly room finally established contact. "Specialist Karns?" asked the chaplain. "Yes sir," said Karns. The chaplain went on, careful not to leave the man hanging in the balance about a possible disaster, "I have a radiogram from your mother; it is not bad news—she is simply wondering how you are getting along. Could you come by the office? I believe we could talk more easily here."

Karns came in, looking a bit shamefaced. There was a twisted sort of half-smile on his lips. The chaplain got up, shook hands, motioned to a seat by the desk and showed him the radiogram. The young man looked up, "Chaplain, my mother is a very nervous person. She worries all the time. I'm not surprised about this radiogram, because you know how the mail was delayed during the typhoon threat. Actually she ought to have received a letter from me by now."

"You have written her recently then?"

"Yes, Chaplain. I did miss a week, and I shouldn't have. You ought to know my mother. She is very nervous. I know this and have tried to be sure to write her regularly."

"You've learned to live with the fact of your mother's nervousness?"

"Yes, I've had to."

"Are you and your mother alone?"

"No sir. My father is at home. He tries to help her, too, but his work keeps him away for much of the time. He travels as a sort of technician for a company that makes and sells oil field equipment. That's another reason why I try to keep Mother feeling at ease. It does make it tough for him when he is home and she is worried about something. Actually, Dad is a real fine guy, but he just has a hard time showing his feelings."

"You feel that your father understands, but due to his long absences and his unemotional nature, he can't help your mother very much with her feelings."

"Yeah . . . I guess that's it."

"Seems like that sort of puts the burden on you . . . right?"

"That's it, all right. And if I drop the ball, then somebody hears from mother."

"It embarrasses you to have to talk to me . . . or anybody . . . about this."

"Well . . . I guess so. Anyway, I hate to take your time. You've got worse problems than mine to deal with. I'll write her again tonight. When I was at home it was easy to keep her happy. But it is awfully hard to do through the mails."

Specialist Karns left. The chaplain had tried to leave the door open for him to return should he feel the need to talk. Now there was an answer to get off to the mother. In the answer the chaplain told Mrs. Karns that he knew she had probably received news from her son by now, but he wanted to let her know that the two had had a good talk and that the boy was in good health and missed his family. He urged the mother to write directly to him whenever she wanted to, and he assured her of an answer. In the letter, he also pointed out that there were often delays due to weather disturbances and that nothing could be done about them. When airmail cannot get through, often the disturbance is such that no overseas calls can be completed, either.

In a short time, the chaplain had an answer apologizing for the fact that she got worried so easily. She said it was much worse now that the boy was so far from home. In answer to her letter, the chaplain tried tactfully to encourage her to see her pastor at home, or her family doctor, if she had one, to seek help for her feelings. No further contact was made.

What the chaplain attempted to do was to make a referral to someone close at hand. If there were qualified professionally trained people she could trust, she might get help not only with present stresses but with her basic problem. Sometimes such attempts are successful. Occasionally the chaplain gets a letter from a pastor-counselor who has picked up one of his referrals. Often a mutual exchange of information is helpful, if it does not deteriorate into simple curiosity or worse. Even if not much help is gained on the matter at hand, it is still important to know that we are not working completely in the dark.

The same approach in reverse often helps. If a minister at home can encourage the family member overseas to seek out his chaplain, or some other professionally qualified person to whom he can talk with confidence, then the positive value of his earlier contacts with the person may be carried over, at least to some degree, to the chaplain.

The Problem of Communication

It is true that separation aggravates problems. Just the fact that close relationships are broken by the miles between makes problems harder to handle. A wife with a husband far away may not be able to get over to him why she is so frustrated by a simple financial matter or, on the other hand, why she does not seem concerned enough by a daughter's illness. If they were together, the matter could be handled, if it needed to be handled at all. Often just being together is all that may be required. Away from home, even the most eloquent words are inadequate. If words are necessary, at home together the questions that push toward clarity can be expressed. Far from home, these questions come through so slowly that the matter requiring clarification is often past history by the time they can be answered. Failure to note the questions in a letter or to consider them worthy of an answer can create a more serious problem than the one that initially stirred up the storm.

Even trained writers wrestle doggedly with the English language to make it speak clearly. Most of us do not have that training, so we cannot expect it to sit up and bark for us just because we happen to want it to do so. If we are only slightly unhappy with our present setup, that is all we need to let our mind select words on the "gray" side. If a letter tinged with gloominess reaches one who is momentarily plunged into depression, then the already weighted words are received as heavy with disaster. If you are feeling lighthearted, it is difficult to give full credit to the apparently trivial worries of a family member far from home; a reply in light vein, however, might be interpreted by the anxious one as utterly callous. The problem of communication is not only a semantic one, it is emotional. Perhaps I should say, borrowing a creation of James Thurber's, it is "psycho-semantic."

A simple parlor game can illustrate something of the problem of communication. Enact a striking scene before a classroom, then ask the class to write down what happened without comparing notes. Then read the varying views of a simple event that took place before their very eyes. You will recognize the problem. Think how difficult it is for lawyers to find out exactly what occurred in a simple, two-car traffic accident watched by two fairly intelligent witnesses from almost the same vantage point, and you will see how the problem shapes up. Imagine the increase in the intensity of the problem if you have two people who are deeply involved emotionally in the "facts" of the case and who are miles away from one another.

It is important that both civilian and military clergymen working with families separated by the demands of the military service realize the shadow world of long-distance communication. The counselor in such cases has to recognize his own problems and strive not to over-react to the written word. He must be able to spot areas of possible misunderstanding and make clear the danger to the counselee. If contact can be established with another counselor working with the distant person it may be helpful but, as will be discussed later, it also opens up a new possibility of even more misunderstanding. Knowledge of the problem is certainly part of the battle. To assume that it is easy to understand and to communicate, and that only the deliberately difficult person refuses to understand is to wreck any chance for help for the persons primarily concerned.

Anxiety and Separation

Let's take a further look at some of the types of both people and problems that add fuel to the fire of poor communication. In Mrs. Karns we met the person whose "free, floating anxieties" attach themselves to any available excuse. As Harry Stack Sullivan has frequently pointed out, anxiety is one state of mind that seems to be intolerable. A person suffering from a basic anxiety about life will work quickly to exchange such formless fears for some other currency. He may move swiftly and without his own knowledge from anxiety to anger or to jealousy or to the irrational fears we call phobias. Some way or other he moves from a nebulous but all-pervading insecurity to a clear-cut feeling that can be pinned down. A basically anxious person may find some of his anxiety relieved by the concern of those close to him and by their willingness to accept him as he is. Remove the source of emotional reassurance from the scene of battle, and the panic associated with anxiety is activated.

Actually such people cannot be placed at ease for long periods of time, even when surrounded by those who care and who are willing to put up with the constant harassment caused by living near them. The family's basic affection for the disturbed one may force them to find indirect and unrecognized ways of handling the matter, but they will handle it. In the case of Mrs. Karns it may be only partly true that "Father" had to take a job as a traveling technician to take care of the family. Father had a good reason for convincing himself such a job was necessary. The father's concern with his job and fatigue from his labors may be real, but there may be secondary gains—he has a good excuse for shifting the burden of reassuring "Mama" to the son. Then came the draft and the son was spirited far away by the needs of the military service. You may be fairly certain that the father was also feeling the stress of separation, for now much of the burden carried by the boy has returned to him. Father may truthfully miss his boy who is overseas, because of his love for him, but the pain of separation is increased by prodding "Papa" to reassume that which he should never have relinquished.

It is not difficult to see what the problem of communication can do to an already anxious person. Such a person will never simply read a letter. He will read into it. In the military the serviceman is told always to "read the problem." He is exhorted not to "fight" the problem or to read into it. This would be a very good rule for the guidance of those whose personal relationships must be maintained through the mails. However, the anxious person simply cannot master this trick. Inevitably he will overreact. The best way to handle the problem would not be to send the parties involved to school to learn how to write letters. It would be to offer the anxious one some form of treatment for his anxiety. That was what the chaplain had in mind when he attempted to encourage Mrs. Karns to see her local pastor. If William Shakespeare, Somerset Maugham, and Ernest Hemingway combined their efforts to write a letter that would preclude misunderstanding on the part of a normal person, to say nothing of a pathologically anxious one, they would inevitably have to admit defeat.

Self-Understanding and Separation

Without buying the whole Freudian bit (which, of course, would be impossible anyway, there being so many varied views among those on whom that label is often placed), it is clear that there are many basic psychic facts about man that display a readiness to put self at the center of the universe. Another way of saying this is to admit that there is something in the religious doctrine of "original sin"—that sin originates in each person anew, and that its basic nature is simply a drive to push God out of the center of the world and substitute "self." Put it another way and you may say that a hungry or love-starved person has no conscience. At least his conscience is not enough to rule out certain desires. His conscience may be strong enough to divert the form of expression of the appetite on the loose, but not to rule out the appetite.

These facts also complicate the problem of separation and make the matter of communication so difficult. For instance, a husband far from home and living in a situation where female companionship for any desired purpose is fairly easy to obtain, may keep himself in line. He may out of loyalty to his wife exercise control. His love for her may be so deep that he really cannot recognize in himself the drive for sexual relief with anyone available. But his drive may express itself another way. He may become overly concerned about his wife's love for him. Her nicely worded letters of well-bred affection may seem cold to him. Any less than ardent expression of her love may cause him to question its existence. It can even get to the point that he begins to suspect his wife. The mechanism at work here may be simply what some call "Projection." At a level beneath his own ability to spot it, the husband is thinking: "What I want to do, she must want to do." Or even, "I cannot admit that I would feel this way, so it must not be me—perhaps it is my wife." And, in the words of the great mass-media philosopher, Jackie Gleason, "Away we go!"

Related to this, but not concerned directly with the problem of communication, is another problem. An individual, male or female, brought up in some corners of our culture even today, grows up feeling that certain things are not to be admitted about man's nature. Man ought to be able to keep himself under control, including even his thoughts. Man can be perfectly good if he only wills it. In theology this is a form of salvation by works. It is a denial that there is much difference between God and man. You should be "like Jesus" is one way this is put. Implied in such a plea from the pulpit or the pew is the idea that "I can be like Jesus. Why can't *you?*" It is also true that this attitude makes a person a sitting duck for the first upsurge of passion that manages to slip by a usually alert censor. When a man begins to feel he can be perfectly good if he only wants to, he loses contact with the fact that the very God he wants to imitate made him a sexual being and built into him a strong appetite. He forgets also that that very God wanted him to live out his allotted days, and therefore put within him a strong desire to go on living, no matter what. True, that same God gave him all he needs to channel these drives into morally acceptable channels—but not without some difficulty. Thus it is normal for a person to feel sexual desire. If we did not, the race would have died out long ago. That urge is not effectively nailed down to only one person. A sense of loyalty toward another and a strong, healthy conscience may accomplish such a feat, but it is a constantly recurring battle.

What I am pointing up here is the fact that some married couples, who would never be greatly affected by such a problem if they were together at all times, have trouble in handling their feelings when they are separated. The miles between affect the biblical injunction to "cleave together and to become one flesh." And so, either the wife or the husband may become conscious of errant feelings of physical attraction toward someone else. With healthy, strong-minded people who can accept themselves even as God accepts them, these problems are seen for what they are, perfectly natural feelings which need not influence action at all. They realize the truth of the tired old saying, "I can't keep the birds from flying over my head, but I can keep them from building their nests in my hair." But those who, for any reason, cannot admit the earthy part of their nature as part of this present condition, may come up with emotional problems. "How could I love my husband, if I let myself have these thoughts" or "How can I believe in myself anymore as a good person if I feel like this?" Such thoughts may have the disastrous effect of centering attention upon the problem. Aware of a problem, we redouble our efforts not to think about it, not realizing that consciously "not-thinking" about a matter is a way of being certain that you think about it. It is like the child's trick statement: "I'll give you $10,000 for not thinking about a rhinoceros for the next thirty seconds." You have already lost.

An alert pastoral counselor can help individuals toward a better understanding of self in the sight of God and thus can alleviate many of these and similar problems. It is my feeling that marriages have been broken and lives ruined because persons troubled with self-accusatory thoughts have not had an opportunity to grow in self-understanding. Such thoughts carried out in logical extension often end in "Since I already feel like this, then why not let go . . . if I am already no good because of my evil thoughts, why don't I go ahead and act out the thoughts." In marriage a failure to understand mature, married love, as opposed to unrealistically understood "romantic" love, can lead to a tragic and most unnecessary divorce. Chaplains overseas and pastors at home can help in many of such cases that come their way. They can help by establishing a relationship of acceptance and understanding (acceptance without understanding may not be enough) in which a counselee may be encouraged and assisted to grow toward a life of realistic adjustment to the finest in human possibilities. Such an adjustment is not a selling out to a baser nature. It is establishing the possibility for further growth in accordance with a God-given nature.

Separation and Growth

Part of the motivation for many marriages is an intricate meshing of immature, or even neurotic, needs. It is not strange that the natural demands for growth which life puts upon us lead to problems with the relationship. Two young people meet at one level of development, and each seems to the other the final fulfillment of all of life. She has been pampered and cared for, the spoiled darling of her parents. He has been struggling to feel capable, aggressive, and truly male. Her dependence upon him for everything made him feel ten feet tall. His willingness to take over and protect made her feel that marriage could be a continuation of the untroubled life she had known. Obviously such a complementary arrangement could not exist for a lifetime. Changes will occur within both of them and adjustments will have to be made on a more realistic basis. There is a time coming when she will have to be strong enough not only to stand alone, but also to take care of the children without constant assistance from him. Sooner or later he is going to need to turn to her for help, emotional or otherwise. The illusion of his infallibility is sure to be dispelled. Somehow he is going to have to develop enough inner security to be able to accept his imperfections and his weaknesses as life makes them evident. When a mutual relationship has been based on attitudes and emotions that are inadequate for life itself, then the individuals concerned must be able to tolerate change within themselves and within one another. If they cannot, then the accusatory phrases are heard: "What happened to the man I married?" "When we first got married you seemed to have a lot more time for love," "I guess I just don't really know you anymore." Even stable marriages existing in the framework of the old hometown have such difficulties. It is not strange that the separation involved in military life makes such adjustments even more difficult.

Sometimes a girl, thrown on her own, is forced to grow and does. She becomes sure of her ability to meet life without the protection of her knight in armor. She is secure within and does not require the constant reassurance of the physical expression of affection. It is a new and exciting world for her. Several things can happen. She can begin to ask, "What do I need with him?" And if, as it often happens, she has unconsciously blamed him for the separation, although rationally she knows it is not his fault, the two may go together. She may feel angry with him for letting her down, and she may add to that the newly discovered fact that her need for him was not as complete as it once appeared to be. Put with these the opportunity to meet new people, and you may have a recipe for trouble. Also, it is often true that she feels the need to go to work to help support the family. Life is always more expensive when the family is operating on two independent budgets. Work itself both builds up her confidence in herself and her sphere of personal contacts. With all of this it is not strange that the marriage is threatened and that a careful, steady course will have to be steered to bring them through such rough water. For help when such marriages must undergo the separation of military service, the skill and compassion of the home pastor and the military pastor will be heavily taxed.

Another way the problem might develop may be seen from the other side of the picture. If the husband's need to feel important has been met by the total dependency of his bride, it may be that any growth toward maturity on her part comes as a real threat to him. He may not understand what is going on, but he is conscious of a threat. Without inner security, the wide-eyed wonder with which he has been beheld by his wife was a medicine he could not do without. A study of their life together would probably bring to light many ways in which he inadvertently (as far as his self-knowledge is concerned) kept her under the waters of dependency. His control of the checkbook, the bank account, and any other financial matters may have been complete not only because of his greater native ability in such concerns, but because he was never willing to give her a chance to learn. He had all the records and she was not trusted to work with them. Now, many miles apart, she has to handle part of the family finances, and she may find out she has a flair for such things. Indeed she may be shrewder about stretching the pennies than he will ever be. Now she has to make fewer calls upon him for help. With such newly found knowledge may be other gains. Now she knows that as a person she does not require quite as much reassurance as to her worth as she had once demanded from him. Maybe the playback of her value, when spread among many, does not have to be so loud as with only one prime source. Her contacts in the workaday world provide all the assurance she needs that she is a person worthy of consideration. Now all of these discoveries may be handled quite well by the wife. She may never question the importance of the marriage. Really, it could even mean more to her. Yet *he* is pushed.

The insecure husband far away from home may even be more in need of wifely assurance as to his importance. In his unit he may be nothing. He may be trying to break in on a new job for which he is not well suited. He may be struggling for acceptance by the men in his unit. He may be puzzled by the oddness of his environment, and he may wonder if he really belongs anywhere. If, while he is going through this interim state of affairs, his wife's mature independence begins to show too clearly, he may leap to the conclusion that she no longer loves him. Wondering how anyone could really love him or believe in him is part of his present problem. If it is difficult for him to see that anyone could need him, he may be only too willing to equate his wife's healthy development with rejection. "I don't believe in myself. How can anyone else believe in me?" he thinks, and his emotional computer comes up with the wrong answer.

Perhaps enough has been said and enough cases provided to illustrate the main point. Separation does aggravate problems. When the military service separates men from familiar persons and settings, certain problems are aggravated. Often the adjustment is easier for the wife at home, for she is still working within known relationships. She goes to the same filling station, has the same dentist, sees the same people at the same church. She still sees many of their mutual friends, and may have her own family nearby. With all of these reinforcements she can face change with more confidence.

On the other hand, the serviceman is miles from home. He may see no one who reminds him of the past. His job is different, his friends are different. The people over him, whose respect he has to earn, are different. He cannot retreat to an island of the familiar. There are no such islands in the strange sea that surrounds him. Of course, he is a man and our culture does tend to equip men with a needed toughness—or at least, it once did. In the midst of loneliness, boredom, and constant insecurity (which is certainly realistic in many parts of the world where our Army, Navy, and Air Force serve today) he may tend to despair. If while he is facing so many demands to adjust, a change comes over those whom he loves the most, no matter how healthy that change may be, he is sure to have problems. The intensity of the problem would depend, obviously, on many factors, but the major factor would probably be his own self-structure—how strong he is as a person.

The work of the chaplain is cut out for him. He must provide, for as many as he can, enough of a bridge to the familiar for them to be able to walk slowly toward firm ground. He is helped in many cases by the relationship of the serviceman to his church at home. If that has been a strong and healthy one, then the chaplain has a big boost. If, as is often the case, the serviceman's understanding of the Church has been based on an experience of judgmental rejection, then the work is going to be more difficult. At any rate, the chaplain must set out to build a relationship of mature trust with the counselee so that the counselee may be enabled to face himself in the presence of another—indeed, in the presence of the God represented by the other. Such a realistic relationship, not based on dependency, involves normal give-and-take and the realization that each man, to a certain extent, must work out his own problems, albeit not alone.

The pastor at home needs understanding of what may be going on within the serviceman, so that his problem can be made clear to the family member at home without impairing respect for the absent one. He must strive to develop a relationship that can be used by the counselee as a means of understanding the changes going on within them and how those changes might be perceived by the absent one. The changes must be recognized, but they must be seen as happening on a framework of continuity. Always must be held up the fact that growth toward maturity ought to be welcomed, no matter how painful the period of transition.

Perhaps a word of warning should be given against a tendency to overpsychologize problems in our time. True, there is much to be learned from looking at behavior and striving to draw out a purpose for all activity. But to do so without humor is to seek trouble unnecessarily. For instance, not long ago a man at an isolated post of foreign duty approached his chaplain. Perhaps the man had read too widely in the psychological folklore of well-known periodicals. What he thought he had learned had him greatly disturbed. He told the chaplain that his wife had begun to show less affection for him in her letters. He felt she had not responded to their love-making when he was at home as she should, and he had wondered then if there was a possibility of frigidity. Since most men pose such a question at one time or another in their married lives, the chaplain was not too convinced of the reality of the problem. Sensing the fact that the intensity of his problem was being discounted, the man produced the final proof. In a letter from his wife, she said that she had a new job and was happier at it than at anything she had ever done. She was selling refrigerators!

Let it be said that separation brings to the surface enough very real problems. It does not take an amateurish dredging of the deeps of the unconscious to find areas of need. Such attempts may only confuse. Basically, what is required in most cases is the common-sense teamwork of the military and civilian clergymen whose work brings them in contact with individuals facing a long period of separation one from another.

CHAPTER FOUR

"MRS. JONES ASKED Me To HELP"

(Co-operating through Correspondence)

Underlining most of the problems that beset military people overseas is the added problem of the miles, and even the months, between the people involved. This problem also thwarts those who are trying to help. For instance, in marital counseling it is now quite generally felt that it is much better, at least for most of the sessions, to see the couple together. To work with individuals only is to perpetuate the rift, indeed to dig the chasm deeper. The goal of marriage counseling is supposedly not the treatment of individuals, but the treatment of the marriage. Where the people are thousands of miles apart, such an approach is obviously impossible. When counselors get together and discuss cases there are many possibilities for distortion, but those possibilities are greatly increased by discussion through the mails. Even if there was plenty of money, telephonic communication from overseas situations is a very shaky thing. Radiograms, or cables, must be too brief to communicate nuances so important in work with people. If counselors feel it is necessary to contact one another in such cases, they must write. Even trained people have much difficulty in forcing the English language to communicate clearly in writing.

Correspondence that Communicates

When two people are talking face-to-face they can sense by facial expressions and by gestures when a matter needs to be restated and approached from a different angle. Questions can be asked and answered, and clarification can be sought as a mutual task. When a man writes, he has in his mind what he thinks he is saying. He feels some things are obvious because they are obvious to him. He cannot detect the shadows of confusion he could see if his correspondent were seated across from him. Writing, after having turned a problem over and over in his own mind, he has forgotten the tortuous steps he had to go through to arrive at his present state of understanding. He expects his reader to leap to conclusions toward which he himself had to crawl. Even when he rereads his letter it still says to him much more than is written down. It takes a supreme act of objectivity to read critically what one has just written. Actually, the letter writer would be much better off if he kept a letter a day, or possibly even two, after he has written it. The time-honored advice to "sleep on it" is actually a very good rule. The next day, the letter that sparkled with incisive insights, that proclaimed with miraculous clarity its message so well that anyone could understand it, often appears muddy, lifeless, and noncommunicative. It may even be worse. It may appear calculated to distort.

Working against such patient consideration of what one has written is the press of the counselor's schedule. If he is to help many, he cannot spend undue time on a few. For the pastor with an over-identification with God, this is even more threatening. If he is the only one who can really help people, then people do not get help unless he sees them. Such being the case, he must move hurriedly. To write a letter at all is quite an accomplishment when one is the only God there is in that part of the world. But even if the pastor has overcome his need to be God, his schedule is quite realistically demanding. Although he may agree it is better to make haste slowly, he is on a treadmill and cannot stop. A pastoral counselor is often worse off than one who is exclusively a counselor by trade. The recognized "counselor" has a heavy schedule, as our civilization tends to produce an unending line of new clients (or old ones back for a patch-up job), but counseling is his business. He does not have to stop to meet with the governing board of his church or hear complaints about moving a morning service from 11 A.M. to 10 A.M. He does not have hospital calls to make, or demanding members who require home visits just because they are lonely. Nor does he have sermons to prepare (although he may have speaking dates to prepare for, they are not so alarmingly regular—he is not squeezed between Sundays). Words are completely tyrannical. They will not yield easily to the demands of common sense. No matter how pressed a man is, words will not march double-time until they feel like it.

So the pastor quickly evaluates the situation and tosses off a letter. Often he fails even to read it over. He may dictate it quickly to a secretary and have her sign it for him. Few military chaplains do that, mainly because they do not have secretaries. They are forced to recheck the work of assistants who may be working with them because the unit didn't want them. There are many chaplain's assistants who are superbly qualified; there are also many more who simply want to get out of all of the field work they might have had elsewhere. And some are would-be ministers who have taken a few Bible courses, whose knowledge of what is necessary may not agree with the chaplain's view. Even the well-motivated may not have had (and usually have not had) stenographic training; their work has to be checked for obvious errors in spelling or in grammar. This deference to reality, forced upon the chaplain, may work to the advantage of those to whom he is writing. Checking a letter over for spelling may also disclose failures to get over what he was trying to say. It may be that the civilian pastor has the same problems with his secretarial help, but whatever the force at work, anything that makes a counselor reread his letters may work to the advantage of his clients.

The Need to Play "God"

Perhaps a word is in order about a matter already discussed, the need to play "God." Those who are being trained to do psychotherapy are warned about the "need to cure." This is the same problem. The psychotherapist who *must* cure gets in his own way. He forces his clients toward his own conclusions. His interpretations are not tentative; they are absolute, no matter how tentatively phrased. If he presents his work at a case conference, he is already prepared to beat down the questions of his colleagues and win the day for his superior "insight." Indeed, to question his work is to question him personally. You cannot simply raise questions for clarification; you are an enemy of the truth if you question at all. Certainly this is seen in the attitude of the all-knowing pastor. The clergyman who knows God's will better than anyone else, including God, will do more harm than good. He will confuse rather than clarify. He will complicate the problem. Certainly he will be unable to communicate, because his preconceptions will distort what he writes.

This problem is rarely seen in its extreme, but I have so stated it to make clear an attitude which at a much more benign level can still distort the written word. Such a clergyman, be he military or civilian, will express himself defensively rather than openly. He will marshal his arguments in such a way as to attempt to propel the reader of the letter to a predetermined action. The writer does not try to convey facts—he tries to get the results he believes he ought to have. He begins his letter "Mrs. Jones asked me to help" and he ends by asking the recipient to be his agent in carrying out a course of action he believes to be right. He may ask the chaplain to call Lieutenant Jones in and "straighten him out." If a financial problem is the symptom that has been presented by the wife, then the chaplain is asked to see the man and have him increase his allotment.

Of course, the chaplain is subject to the same error. Many times chaplains write in such a way that it becomes obvious that they consider the home pastor to be nothing more than an agent to do for them what they would do if they were in the home setting. It seems to be a disease of clergymen to assume that they are the only ones who know what ought to be done.

In a psychiatric case conference a group of residents and some senior staff men were lectured by a famous visitor. The speaker, a specialist in group therapy, observed that psychiatrists often do not simply want a person to get better—they must get better their way. If Dr. Owens helps a patient, symptomatic relief is all that is achieved. *I* must help or no help is to be received. No *real* help, that is. The speaker's point was that if doctors are threatened by the successes of other doctors, it is scarcely surprising that a group concept recognizing that even sick laymen can help other sick laymen is under professional attack.

Here is the problem of the clergyman who thinks his thoughts are God's thoughts. He really does not want his parishioners to get help. He wants them to be helped only by himself. Only *his brand* of salvation is true salvation. Only the advice *he* offers is truly objective and ultimately valid. Where such an attitude exists, even to a small degree, the ability to consult with other counselors through the mail may be dangerously affected.

Part of the same problem is our tendency to lack trust in one another. Professional counselors or psychotherapists have their troubles in communication, but they do at least have certain accepted standards of training. They can assume, if they know that the man they are writing is recognized in the field, that he is qualified to do his own thinking based on the facts they convey. The civilian clergyman who writes to the military chaplain overseas has no way of knowing what use will be made of what is conveyed. The reverse of the problem is also true. Having known clergymen with little understanding of human problems, one is not too ready to trust an unknown man completely. Having seen lives hurt unnecessarily by high-handed declaimers of God's will, it is not strange that openness of communication is lacking in many letters. Yet we must defer to the facts. Whether or not we can know the man to whom we write, we must write as professionally as we can. I am responsible only for doing the best job I am qualified to do. If I do my work well and someone else fails, I cannot berate myself for failure.

How to Communicate

Now what does it mean to do my work well in this matter? It means that I must limit myself to what my parishioner allows me to write. It means I must be ethically bound to recognize his right to a privileged communication. I must never write facts about another's life that he is not prepared to release. It means also that I must recognize the limits of my own knowledge. I can know very little about people I have known all my life. What makes me think I can know all there is to know not only about a person I have seen but a few times but also all about the wife or husband miles away, whom I may never have seen at all? I must be willing to state, with some objectivity, the facts which I feel bear upon the case. Even if I am in doubt about the applicability of some information which my client has asked me to convey, I am bound to include it for my correspondent. I must defer to his ability to use good judgment. I must be detailed enough to be helpful but must learn to be as brief as possible. It may take me a little longer to write a brief letter that covers the subject, than to ramble for page after page, but it is necessary for me to do so. I must also refrain from using my faraway colleague as an extension of my arms and legs. He is not to become an ecclesiastical errand boy for me. I must not tell him exactly what he is to force another to do. I must present the facts, and in so doing I must state how these "facts" came to my knowledge. Are they simply what my parishioner told me to be true, or are they gleaned from personal observation? I can and must recognize that I am not doing a client a disservice by recognizing that his statements of "fact" may well be colored by his involvement. Certainly I must know that a hurt wife or husband, even when striving desperately to be objective, cannot help but distort the problem. I can still honor a person as truthfully feeling that what he says is true, even when his statement turns out to be shot with error. So I must learn to point out the source of my "facts" when I write to another counselor.

Why Bother?

What is stated here about co-operating by correspondence is not to be taken as any recommendation that the writing of letters is superior to face-to-face communication. All I am doing is bowing to the facts of life. Many people who see a pastor or a chaplain will get no help at all if letters are not written. Thousands of miles away from one another and facing many months of such a separation, all that remains is the written word. Perhaps that written word, clarified by personal conferences with an available civilian or military pastor, will be all that is needed in some cases. Certainly it is worth a trial. Where the counselor is trained, his work will be of much more assistance than trying to handle the matter only by exchanges of letters between those who are directly involved. Letters between the two, plus letters between counselors, augmented by personal sessions between the chaplain and the husband and the civilian pastor and the wife (or vice versa), are necessary if help is to be received. Such an approach is the only possible one in many circumstances.

It must be remembered that, although the Government of the United States has tried to cover certain emergencies by regulations making leave possible, or even providing in some carefully documented cases for discharge, or for transfers closer to home, there are many situations that are perceived as real emergencies by those involved but are not covered. Economically and logistically it is impossible to cover every case. Remembering also that emergencies tend to equate with the possibilities under regulations, the problem is seen as even more difficult. Face it. In most of the cases handled by clergymen, there will be no transfer, no discharge from the service, and no leave. Help will have to be offered within the realistic context of a long-term separation. The two clergymen, military and civilian, must learn to be as helpful as possible in a co-operative venture through the mails. No one likes this, but it is a situation that must be lived with.

Other Considerations

It is my feeling that clergymen might well exchange some information in verbatim style, reporting conversational exchanges as closely as possible to the way they happened. The counselor who receives such a report is then left to consider and observe. In some instances he might be able to spot possible errors in technique on the part of the writer. I know that some will recoil in horror and feel that trouble is being invited. I share the feelings of others in the field: that we who counsel must develop the same thick skins that are required of medically trained people. We must be strong enough to open ourselves to criticism, or we may never learn to be as helpful as we should be. This does not mean that I must agree with any critique that is offered me. I must simply evaluate such comments professionally and determine whether or not they indicate a change in approach. It may be that I will alter my course of action. It may be that I will simply be confirmed as to my first judgment. But nonetheless I have been willing to risk "feelings" in the interest of helping others.

As recording devices become more and more an instrument of good pastoral counseling, I believe that the time will come when tapes will be exchanged through the mails between counselors. Tapes are being exchanged by families that are separated by the miles. Why could not counselors, with the consent of the counselees, do likewise? When the voice with all of its variations of tonal quality, pitch, and emphasis is available, then much more can be learned than when only the inscrutable, enigmatic, and utterly unmanageable written word is before us.

At least one other pitfall should be pointed out to those who must counsel and confer through the mails. This is the problem of over-identification. Such a problem exists in all counseling, but the danger is even more pronounced when there is no possibility of contact with anyone other than the person who is seeing you. Observing the emotional tension that besets our counselee, we feel compassion. Compassion is a God-given emotion, but like all God-given things, it can become demonic. If compassion leads us to become so much one with the sufferer that we suffer to a like degree, we may only contribute to the problem. We do not help, when we are only a pale shadow of the feelings of those with whom we work. We need compassion enough not to let compassion obscure our view of the real needs of those we would help. We do not help by seeing the other party to the problem as a callous beast, even if that is the way our counselee sees him. We must learn to assist our counselee to recognize and understand his feelings and his own participation in the problem. We must learn to keep the focus on him while we are with him. We do no good if we begin to join forces in a battle against the absent one. Since the only one we can help is the one who is with us, let us learn to help him accept as much of the responsibility for the problem as is his. We can be certain that even in clear-cut cases of injustice, the injured one has in some way added to the problem. So often letters are received wherein it is clear that the counselor at home has already decided that the absent party is the culprit who must be forced to co-operate. Pastors at home receive letters from military pastors that indicate the chaplain (who, like his client, is a long way from home) has accepted the views of the serviceman without question. The wife is maliciously determined to take advantage of the absence to drive the soldier out of his mind and break up the marriage. The only thing wrong with such involvement is that it robs us of the ability to help. I do not sit in moral judgment on such overidentification. I simply point it out as a potentially destructive development. This type of identification could be spotted if verbatim reports were exchanged. If not full verbatims (which time would not permit) certainly extracts of conversational dialogue might help one clergyman-counselor point out to another the evident danger. The most helpful attitude involves enough compassion to understand and to care, and enough objectivity to feel the same way toward the absent party. Compassion plus professional objectivity is required in these cases. Awareness of the danger is already part of the victory. To be unaware of the possibility of overidentification is to compromise the ability to help.

How to Handle Letters in Counseling

In actually handling situations involving counseling by mail, there are certain procedures I believe to be helpful. First, let us consider the case as it often develops. A man comes to the chaplain with a letter from home. He hands it to the clergyman to read. Obviously emotionally involved, he does not trust himself to read the letter to the chaplain. Personally, even where an emotional struggle is clearly going on within the counselee, I find it most helpful to take the letter, but to ask him to tell me what is in it. If after he strives to tell me what he saw in the letter, I feel it necessary to read it, I do so in front of him. By asking him to tell me I force him to work with his feelings.

If you can register understanding, you can help lower the level of tension. Accept feelings, do not fight them. Trust to the facts of counseling experience. You will best help him with his feelings if you allow him to struggle to express them. *Your* reaction to the letter, anyway, is not what is at issue. If the session develops, as it often will, so that you never take time to read the letter, it may be just as well. If you do feel it necessary to read it, do so carefully trying to see it as it must have hit him. To read it and to say, "Look, I read the same letter you did and I don't see the problem," may be logically all right, but emotions ignore the laws of logic. It is best to select phrases throughout the letter and ask what these meant to him. "How does that strike you?" is better than "I don't see why you are so troubled." Such questions can be followed with, "Tell me about it," or by simply using the therapeutic nod of the head or grunt. What is needed is to give him an opportunity to go to work with his feelings. After feelings are dealt with, often matters that once appeared hopeless will seem much less threatening.

In handling letters from other counselors, read carefully, watching for your own reactions and asking yourself why you respond as you do. Read to see where the writer has slipped from objectivity into his own feelings. Note carefully the sources for statements. Were these unsupported statements by the counselee at home or overseas? Are the facts documented? Are they expressions of symptomatic reactions, or do they strike to the heart of the problem? Above all *do not* let the letter move you to a definite mind-set about the problem. True, you can call a man in and lecture him, if you wish—but this is not counseling. Also it is foolish to think you have the answer because you have a letter from someone who thinks he has the answer. Life is much more complex than that. Honor the letter. Do not sit in judgment on the writer, but approach the man with an open mind. Give him a chance to air his feelings toward the absent party and toward you for confronting him with the situation. Don't be thrown by the fact that he may feel hostile toward you. Better hope that he *can* admit it, so that the feelings can be dealt with. Even statements like,

"I'm sure you don't like to be called in like this. . . . I wouldn't either, but I have to send back some sort of answer," may help. Such statements tend to draw off the poison and enable a helping relationship to grow.

The counselor's most helpful attitude is to give his undivided attention to the feelings of the person with whom he is dealing. With such an attitude most problems can be rather quickly approached. If the counselor has already jumped to conclusions established by the writer, his approach to the "culprit" will only drive the conflict underground.

I am not saying that problems exist only in the realm of feelings. Financial problems are financial problems. Sexual unfaithfulness is a real breach of trust. Family strife is a fact of life. Sometimes advice is needed. Clients need to be referred for legal advice or for medical opinions. Realistic and factual problems often need to be handled directly. But even when the matter seems best resolved by advice from a more experienced person, there is still work to be done in the realm of the feelings. Life is not a matter of adding up a balance sheet of arguments for, comparing it with arguments against, and arriving at a solution of the problem. If counseling were a matter of advice-giving and shrewd manipulation of the client toward a pre-conceived "right" course of action, then counseling would be a simple matter indeed. I always remember the words attributed to an old doctor in a medical school in Germany. He was supposed to have written the problem "two plus two" on the blackboard. He drew the line underneath and then stopped. "In arithmetic, two plus two is four," he said, "but when you are dealing with people, two plus two may sometimes be six, or eight, or often, three, but it is *never* four."

Conclusion

Granted counseling by mail and conferring with colleagues by mail is an inadequate approach to human problems. Granted that even in written exchanges of those who know one another intimately, misunderstandings occur. Granted such misunderstandings develop even when the content of the letters is emotionally neutral. Add to the situation an area of relationship that is full of feelings, and meanings naturally become distorted. Bring to the problem letters from clergymen, military and civilian, who know almost nothing about the two involved and who know nothing about one another, and you are certainly on shaky ground. Yet it is the nature of our work, that since no other alternative is available, we must step out, however uncertain the ground. The one alternative that might occur to others is to refuse to try to help at all. Such an alternative is not a live option for the clergyman.

The complex nature of the problem has been pointed out not to frighten chaplains and civilian clergymen away, but because it is necessary to recognize the nature of the beast before we grapple with it. To be aware of the many possibilities of confusion and distortion, is to be well armed to cope with them. To recognize the frustrations that inevitably accompany such attempts to help, is to take the sting out of them. We will often fail. But it won't be because we failed to try.

The clergyman who would try must be ready to live with frustration without wallowing in self-blame. I recall one example from the many I have accumulated through the years. The first letter I received was mailed to me from a chaplain who had originally been brought into the problem. He had received a letter from a pastor in the States, and he had had one session with the man concerned. He had handled the factual side of the problem, he thought, and had dismissed the matter. The solution decided upon had later been rejected by the serviceman, without a word to the chaplain. The second letter came from the home pastor and was forwarded to the chaplain, who had since been transferred. The letter finally was sent to me. By then the man concerned was away on a special assignment far from contact with any chaplain. A letter to him had to be carried by courier. When he returned I was away and he had left again by the time I returned. In the next letter from the States the negative feelings the home pastor had toward me and the man were clearly evident. Much time had elapsed. Problems may become less threatening, or more so, by the mere passage of time. This one evidently was more so for the wife at home. But nothing else could be done.

I think the point is clear. In counseling by mail across the miles and across the months, frustration is the norm. But the other point is also clear. A conscientious clergyman can not allow himself the luxury of deciding not to try. Be warned of the difficulties ahead, but move out smartly.

CHAPTER FIVE

"I HAVE NEWS For YOU"

(Grief Work with the Serviceman and His Family)

It was getting close to sundown and the chaplain still had about two hours of riding before him. Both he and his driver were anxious to get home. However, he remembered that the wife and children of one of the men in his unit lived in the community near the hospital where he had been visiting. He gave his driver directions and began thinking ahead to the next Sunday. Still preoccupied when they drove up in front of the house where the family lived, he jumped from the jeep without thinking and "lit running." His only thought was to make the visit and go home. Suddenly he realized that the woman, who had recognized him as he drove up, had come out to meet him. His hurried steps had alerted her to unspoken fears. Her husband had been hurt . . . or even, killed! Her expression reflected her inner fears. The chaplain saw the shock she was experiencing and quickly understood. She was seeing him as the bearer of bad news. He quickly clarified. "Nothing is wrong. I just wanted to see you—to stop by for a visit."

Even as he spoke he realized how he had failed. The thoughts and feelings triggered by an unexpected visit from a man of the cloth had been ignored. Thinking of himself as a pretty good "Joe," he had quite forgotten the impact of the role of the clergyman. The chaplain finds out about his role in many ways. People talking happily together, quickly change the subject when he arrives. Laughter drifts off into silence. A heavy formality comes over the group. A visit to a sick man in the hospital brings the probing, half-joking query, "Am I that bad, Chaplain?" The visit the chaplain was making on a serviceman's family had simply brought a normal response. As a military chaplain, he had failed by not thinking about the impact he was making when he jumped from the jeep and walked quickly toward the door. The frown on his face was only the result of his preoccupation with future plans, but it was interpreted as an announcement of despair. A clergyman, civilian or military, must never forget the implications of his role. No matter how he views himself as a person, he carries the weight of centuries of experience on his shoulders. Certainly it is a wise idea for him to structure the nature of his call. A quick statement, "Hi, I just came by to see how things were going" or "I just wanted to say Hello," will allay needless fears. The psychic shock borne by the serviceman's wife in this case was a real one, and she should not have been required to experience it.

How to Deliver Bad News

Since in the military there are fewer sources of bad news than in a community full of friends and relatives, the work of carrying bad news falls even more often upon the chaplain. Commanders expect him to deliver death notices to servicemen and dependents. Often parents ask the American Red Cross to have the message delivered by the chaplain. And this is a work that does not inspire much competition. People are usually not jealous of their right to deliver bad news. It is a work which more often than not falls on the chaplain. He must learn to do a difficult job as well as possible. There is no sugar-coating of the fact that it is a bitter, mean job. There is no way of avoiding the fact, however, that it must be done, and that the chaplain should be the best man to do it. Hometown pastors might well advise their people to request that such messages be delivered by the chaplain of the serviceman's unit. A statement as to the denominational affiliation of the man would help the chaplain who must do the work.

The delivery of such a message is never easy. To me it is somewhat like talking to a man in a friendly way and, without warning, while looking him straight in the eye, slugging him viciously in the stomach. I have seen big men drop heavily into a chair or onto a cot, gasping for breath, after receiving bad news. While there is no easy way to handle the job, there are some suggestions that make sense for any clergyman called to perform such a task. First, try to pick your spot. Seek a place that is private, cut off from view, and that provides seating for at least the one who is to be told. Second, ask him to sit down, even if only on the edge of a cot. Work quickly, for the questions that throng to a man's mind are pressing and weigh heavily upon him. Anxiety is itself a heavy blow. Doubt is its own burden. Move quickly from the unknown to the known to prevent a painful prolongation of anxiety.

Third, give him the information in small segments, allowing just enough time for him to assimilate what he has heard. When the mind is crowded with fear, it cannot absorb much at a time. Remember, the man has already begun to react to the fact of misfortune. Don't wait too long, and don't use unnecessary words. Be brief and to the point. This outline may seem overly mechanical, but it works. Tell him somewhat in this order: "I have news for you." Pause briefly. "It is not good news." Then quickly add, "It is about your brother." Pause briefly. "He's dead."

The pauses are actually only fragments of seconds. The idea is that when a man is carrying a heavy load of anxiety he can only understand short, clear statements. After each statement the mind quickly seeks to adjust. It absorbs bit by bit and builds up its readiness for the next. By the time the final information is given, a lot of psychic work has been done. After many conversations with other chaplains and with Red Cross men, many of whom are most perceptive, it is my belief that the above, or some slight modification of it, presents the best possible way of doing a difficult job well.

It does not work to hit a man suddenly with the total information. He is not ready for it. It is like dropping a load of bricks on him. He needs time to prepare his muscles for the burden. But the other side is true also. Don't wait too long to get the entire message out. In most cases he is already jumping to a more catastrophic conclusion than the facts allow. If you are telling him that an uncle died, he has already assumed it was his wife or his mother. If you are telling him that his mother died, he has guessed that it was both his mother and father and all of his brothers and sisters. Once you set out to give a man bad news, make it impossible for him to make it worse than it is. When you say, "I have news," he tenses. With "It is not good," he is tied in knots. "It is about your brother," then he really knows. When you say, "He died," then the load has been delivered. Now give him time to deal with it. Now you can afford to take the time to tell him something like this, "I know this is rough. Don't feel that you have to say anything. I'll sit here quietly with you for a few minutes. Then we can talk if you want to." After a statement such as this, the chaplain should steel himself to sit there quietly. No man is at ease after having told another of the death of a family member. The chaplain has activated many fears and doubts within himself. He has been told that he should have faith, that he should see death as a doorway into life. He has heard a long series of such bromides through the years. Yet he is human and death is death. Man has within himself a refusal to think of himself as mortal. He really cannot accept death, and to be pushed by it is to become nervous. Such nervousness causes a man to talk. If the chaplain is not careful he will begin to spout words of "hope." Nothing is more offensive to a man in the first throes of grief than "hope." All such words do is to convince the bereaved one that the chaplain simply does not understand what he is facing. The mourner is already going through an experience of rejection. Life has thrust him out into the cold reaches of eternity. He knows that he is alone. To have someone fail to understand the psychic bleakness of the moment is to have that aloneness emphasized.

It is difficult for a man to cry. Our culture does not allow it. There are enough Spartan overtones in our civilization for it to be made difficult for men to express emotion. The strong, silent "John Wayne" type is still our sentimental idol. Yet it is important that a man express his grief in some way. A word from the chaplain at such a moment can help, but only a quick word, such as, "You and I are alone here. If you want to cry, go ahead. No one else knows." Sometimes I have found it helpful to go even farther and, when it is obvious that the grief is acute and it is difficult for him to express it, to say, "You must have loved her very much." Or, "You must have been very close to him." The idea is to make the loss explicit and to allow the expression of grief. Here it becomes evident why it is necessary to find a place away from others. It is healthful for a man to admit grief and give expression to it, but only when it is done in a nonthreatening environment. To break down in front of his whole platoon might be so damaging that it overbalances the good that might have come from expressing grief. Find a place where only the two of you will be, even if it delays passing on the message. An empty barracks, if you know it will be empty while you need it, is fine. An office away from busy activity might be better. A closed door shuts out the world effectively, but it is even better if the man does not have to go out into feverish activity and walk the gauntlet of many inquisitive eyes.

While serving as a hospital chaplain it was necessary for me to meet a plane to deliver a death message to a mother who had only been informed that her son was seriously ill. She had been in the air when the boy died, and there had been no way of informing her. I took the hospital commander's sedan and started for the airport. The airport itself had only one tiny building with no office space at all. There was no quiet room for the delivery of the message. I knew that the mother was hoping to be with her boy for a while, and even with death inevitable, it is comforting to have had a final visit. That visit was to be denied. I knew the moment was fraught with tragedy. I also knew I could not wait to get her back to the hospital to tell her. The best I could do was to get rid of the driver by sending him to get the baggage and advising him not to come back until he was told. Then I met the plane and took the woman quickly to the sedan, which was parked away from other cars. I opened the door. We got in and sat down. Then I delivered the message and stayed with her during the first moments of grief. After her first tentative adjustment to the news, I left her alone while I found the driver. The point is that there is almost always some way of providing a moment of privacy at such a difficult time.

Prayer and Grief

To this point I have said nothing about prayer. Prayer must not be a nervous reaction on the part of the chaplain. It must not be offered as a way of helping the chaplain handle his feelings. Death, of course, forces us to recognize our human condition. Any illusions we have of security are shattered by death. It is normal in such a condition to want to do something that makes us feel at least somewhat in control. A clergyman, who may occasionally confuse himself with God, is threatened by death in a peculiar way. Not knowing what to do, he feels that he must do *something*, or the grief-stricken one will know that he is not infinite but, on the contrary, quite human. So he gets overly encouraging or he prays. His prayer often fails to deal realistically with the needs of the mourner, because unconsciously he is dealing with his own fears.

It has been suggested by many in the field that there are certain signs to look for before offering prayer. These signs are: (1) Are you accepted as a clergyman by the person you are with?; (2) Has the conversation up to this point been phrased in the commonly accepted language of religion?; and (3) Is the person you are with facing a quite serious situation? If all signs are present, the clergyman has forfeited his role if he does not pray. If any two are present, prayer is probably indicated. And if the third sign is quite predominant, prayer probably should be offered. If the situation is threatening enough, even the agnostic wants prayer. He may later reject it as a sign of momentary weakness, but as a frightened human being he wants prayer at that time. All the more reason why it is a good idea to be away from prying eyes in a quiet private place.

The prayer as offered should accept realistically the facts of the situation. It should incorporate the rebellious doubts that are normal to a man faced by the loss of a loved one. It should recognize that God accepts such rebellions as natural for His children. There should be no opportunity left for the person to blame himself later for his outcry against "deaf heaven." But the prayer should also recognize the promise of faith as a later source of real help. Thus, a prayer of this nature can be helpful to a bereaved person:

O God, in this time of darkness we remember Thy Son upon the Cross. We hear echoing in our hearts His cry, "Why hast Thou forsaken me?" and we know, despite our pain, that finally we will be sure "Thou hast not forsaken us," even as Thou didst not forsake Him. Grant to John, in this time of grief, the knowledge that he is not alone, and that the prayers of many are voiced for him. In the lonely days ahead grant to him the strength that comes from the knowledge that Thou dost understand. Make Thy consolation real for him and lead him through this darkness into the light of a new day. This we pray even through Christ our Lord. Amen.

Later prayers can assist in dealing with other problems involved in grief, but one should not attempt too much in the first moments. The prayer given above has the disadvantage of being too long, but it does show human understanding and it does refer beyond human understanding to the constant love of God. Probably the best prayers in the works of a contemporary author are those of Russell Dicks in several of his writings. One should read widely in the language of prayer from the early Church fathers to writers of this present "psychological" age. Steeped in the language of prayer one finds the necessary words.

In this discussion of prayer I am looking primarily at it from the human side. I do not believe that prayer is simply a technique or a mechanical gimmick. I also believe with Paul that we do not know how to pray as we ought. I further believe that the use of the language that has been part of the Christian tradition so long and that demonstrably in the past has opened up channels for God's direct ministry to his lonely ones, is proper. Whatever happens from God's side is up to Him. But certainly we are charged with the responsibility of doing as well as we can that which we can see and know ought to be done.

Facing the Fact of Death

All that has been dealt with thus far in this chapter has been simply the delivery of the message and the few moments following. Certainly much more is to be done, but the effectiveness of what follows is greatly affected by how the first moments are handled. Actually those few moments will influence many hours of thought on the part of the bereaved, and even if the chaplain makes no further contact with that person for some reason, his groundwork can be helpful through many years. The reverse is also true. To bungle the job is to make it difficult for the bereaved and for anyone who must work with him later. To gloss over the very real facts of grief and its implications is to lay the groundwork for trouble. To deal with death unrealistically, and to use a combination of chemicals and so-called "spiritual" bromides is to set up a tragically complex delayed grief reaction. The need to do the work of mourning at the appropriate time is well known. To evade the issue at the time of the loss is to hurt the bereaved person much more over a long period of time than to allow and even to encourage the expression of grief in the early moments after the loss is known. As the surgeon must inflict a wound if the forces of healing are to be released, so must a clergyman learn to hurt another when the facts require it. The compassion with which the work is done will offer some realistic alleviation of the necessary pain.

Much has been written specifically about grief. Some have expanded the topic to include similar reactions caused by separation, whether by the miles or by divorce. It is true that grief is partly a "separation" reaction. The central fact is that the bereaved one is separated from the dead by the grave. This is indisputable. It is also true that there is very real separation caused by the miles that lie between a soldier overseas and his family at home. It is clear that when there is a rift with a loved one, there is emotional separation. It is true that all of these reactions have separation in common. However, I believe there is nothing quite like the finality of separation by death. In recent years it has been pointed out that the separation involved in a soldier's assignment can lead to such complete grief that in some cases the lonely wife or husband tends to "die" to the distant spouse. Yet, I believe that more often than not such language only invites the immature mind to come up with a good Freudian excuse for what is essentially only "hot pants," and not to be dignified by learned psychological phrases.

At any rate, in these pages I am not concerned with drawing out a detailed understanding of grief. A good working volume for such a purpose is *Ministering to the Grief Sufferer* by C. Charles Bachmann, already published in this series. There are many articles and chapters on the grief reaction, most of them depending heavily on the work that was done by Eric Linderman, M.D. after the Coconut Grove fire in Boston, Massachusetts before World War II. The reader is referred to these and other sources for a more comprehensive study of the field. It is my desire to deal with the subject as it relates to our work with servicemen and their families particularly.

The Work of Mourning and the Military Life

After the message of grief has been delivered, much remains to be done. As has often been observed, it takes at least six to ten hours of somebody's time just to listen compassionately while the grief-stricken one mourns. This listening involves certain techniques, such as assisting in making the grief specific by encouraging small talk about the dead one. "You must have had a wonderful time walking together in the garden you told me of," is an example of the kind of focus that is helpful. Also it involves recognizing the normal guilt that plagues the mind of the bereaved. "I only wish I hadn't said what I did the last time I saw her," and other similar statements must be faced and dealt with realistically. No one ever lived closely to any one of us for a period of time without being hurt. This is true, and faced realistically it does no damage, but overly sentimentalized due to the impassable chasm of death, it can wreak havoc. It must be handled. Such listening also involves the gentle redirection of interest toward the living and toward the world we must continue to live in. But all of these matters have been dealt with elsewhere.

The life of the military does add complications. The soldier's life is one of almost endless activity. He has little time to talk. The chaplain has to learn to take advantage of the fleeting moments that are offered. He tries to be available in the field when the soldier is waiting for the next move of his unit. He drops by and makes himself a target for the soldier's thoughts. When it applies, he even lets himself be the focus of the man's hostility toward God. If the chaplain knows such reactions are normal and that, even if expressed as charges against him personally, they are to be accepted and not to be answered, he can help immeasurably. His work may be one that has its unpleasant moments, but the goal he seeks makes it all worth it. If one individual can be helped through the time of grief and can be restored to a vital relation with man and God, then the trouble is all worth it. If the chaplain does not feel like this, then it is possible that he should seek gainful employment in some other line.

What has been said may seem to be pointed primarily at the military chaplain, but it should assist the civilian pastor in understanding something of the problems of his parishioner in the service. Such an understanding has helpful implications for his work with the family at home. Should the time come for the civilian pastor to carry the message of a serviceman's death to his family at home, the principles are still valid. The problem is complicated by separation. As has been observed, there are already certain similarities between death and separation for other reasons, so it is not strange that when the two are superimposed the problem becomes more difficult. It is much harder to face a loss realistically when one is not present at the time. All the more reason for the pastor to work at assisting to objectify the loss. He must provide an opportunity for the grieving one to talk specifically about the dead. Perhaps he needs to make more time available for those service families than for others facing the experience of loss. Separation adds often to the sense of guilt also. The wife may think, "If only I had been willing to join him," "If only I had not let the realistic problem of lack of funds stand in my way," "If only I had written more often," "If only I had offered him my physical love more unrestrainedly," and so on. She can trap herself in the darkness of a forest of "ifs," unless the pastor, or someone, helps her accept her fallible human nature.

And, having faced the problem once, the unfortunate truth is that in many such cases the work will all have to be done again when the body arrives and the funeral is held. If the preliminary work was well done, the newly opened wound will heal rapidly. However, the pastor is warned that the time he gave earlier may have to be repeated when the body is there to be dealt with.

Another problem the home pastor faces is the return of a serviceman or the dependent of a serviceman from overseas after there has been a death in the family at home. No matter how good a job the chaplain has done, the returned family member will want to know the details. "Was she in much pain?" "Did she ask for me?" "I just couldn't come, you know I couldn't!" These, and other questions must be handled in the same spirit that grief counseling is done at any time. Here again it is clear that the person coming back from a distant place is struggling to finish the work of mourning. The pastor is the best one to help. He may want to suggest that they talk to the doctor, particularly if he knows the doctor and knows him to be an understanding person. But he should be ready to do the work, even though he may already have gone through it all with those family members who were at home when it happened.

The very nature of the military life sets up certain problems of which civilian pastors should be aware. For instance, when the serviceman husband dies while still in harness, the wife is plummeted into a new world. Perhaps she has followed her husband from military post to military post for many years. She has so turned her thinking towards her husband's work that she is at home only with military people. In the military community, she has worked hard to make young wives feel at home. She has tried to learn the requirements of protocol as to entertainment. She has supported every charitable work sponsored by the units her husband has served. She is a military wife in every respect. Her emotional capital is invested in her husband's work. But, nonetheless, it is his life and not hers. She is not a member of the military, no matter how long she has been with them. When her husband dies, there is no place for her any longer in the military. If she is living in quarters on post, she is bound to clear them as soon as possible and seek shelter elsewhere. She does not have the time to sort out her husband's belongings and mourn over them until the pain becomes only a constant shadow in the background. She does not have the solace of old friends across the street or next door. She has got to move out into what, for her, is an alien world.

It may be that she moves to what was once their old hometown. More often than not she really doesn't know where to go. She married him while he was in the service and they have moved about like dry leaves over the landscape, putting no roots down. They had not even been able to decide where they wanted to go when he retired. She is forced to go somewhere but does not know where to go. During the work of mourning it is difficult to make sound decisions. Yet she must decide, and the decision she must make is a very important one. She may not have enough money to remedy the situation if she finds that she has made a mistake.

With such people, the civilian pastor has an important role. The military chaplain stays in his environment. He may grieve over the pain he knows she feels, but he can only stay in contact through the mails. If the church people of the community can be alerted to the needs of such women, a truly redemptive work can be accomplished. If the pastor understands what she is facing, he can do much of the work. And his leadership can accomplish the rest. The chaplain has the responsibility to strive to notify the appropriate pastor. Often, however, he cannot know whom to tell. The pastor will come upon the woman through her move toward the church. If he knows that a military widow has visited his church, he should be aware of the peculiar nature of her problem. He must find the way to bring her into the community in a helpful way. It may be that he has in his church school a group of women who, too, have lost their husbands. Such is the way of American life. Perhaps they have enough in common with her to be able to minister to her effectively. Even if they did not have the problem of the need to seek out a new environment and meet strange people, they nonetheless had the pain of loss. They can envision how much worse it could have been in her situation. Their compassionate hearts can also understand her need for dignity, her need not to be patronized. Yet they can sensitively relate her to activities that are needed in the community. They can put her in touch with like minds. They can enfold her in the love of the people of God. And they would not lose by so doing. The rich variety of her experience, her knowledge of strange lands and different ways—all of these would make her an asset to any group. The pastor will also think of the added value she would have to a parish that has many families with loved ones in the military service. Her knowledge of the problems and advantages of the military life would be most helpful in dealing with those families. She could add a touch of realistic familiarity, where before all the family could muster was the construction of anxious imaginations. But whether or not there were any advantages at all in having such a person in the parish, the work of ministering to a grieving heart is our work, and it must be done.

Conclusion

Enough has been said to point out certain peculiar problems service people face in handling grief. Within the military community of the past the matter was handled quite well. Tradition made sure of it. When a unit is a fighting unit, it exists to live. The enemy is to die. We are to live. Thus nothing is said about death. But death comes. Then, in order to do the work of the living, it must be dealt with. This they knew. The old formal military funeral faced this fact and provided the opportunity for quick but effective grief work. The horse with the empty saddle. The empty boots making their last trip. The doleful music of the band. The volley of shots over a comrade's grave. The last clear notes of "Taps" floating over the cemetery. Here is a perfect way to objectify the loss, to encourage the expression of grief, to advance the work of mourning. And then, once done, the quick march of the band, and the unit closes ranks to move on. In this dramatic enactment are all the seeds for a work on the pastoral care for the bereaved. For this is what we must all accomplish when faced with loss. We must admit it. We must express it. We must do as the military—close ranks and move on. The world of the living is our world as long as we are in it. God expects us to do a good job here as long as we can.

CHAPTER SIX

"HE'S A GOOD MAN . . . WHEN HE'S SOBER"

(Alcohol and the Serviceman)

"He's a good man when he's sober, Chaplain, but when he's drunk, he's impossible. And, as a matter of fact, he's drunk most of the time these days."

Alcohol and Our Culture

Many times the chaplain hears these or similar words. They are simple and to the point and can be repeated in a matter of seconds, but behind them there are hours upon hours of tragedy. Any pastor knows this. Alcoholism and problem drinking are increasing among both men and women in our nation. Problems related to compulsive or to simple "heavy drinking" add up to the nation's number one health, marital, and economic problem. In many cases where other patterns of action are at the heart of the problem, alcohol is right there adding to the confusion and multiplying the tragic aspects of any situation. Both civilian and military clergymen are equally well acquainted with these problems. The chaplain to industry is often almost snowed under by problems related to the unrestrained use of alcohol. So many man-hours each year go down the drain due to hangovers, or protracted binges, that management has to be concerned. Since so many of the men involved are those who could be described as "good men when sober" it can be seen that management is not simply concerned out of good will, but out of desperation as well. The man engaged in the battle of the bottle often has a compulsive drive toward perfection, and thus makes a good man in a competitive culture. The fact that his obsession with perfection is based primarily on a lack of faith in himself (which is why he must win external approval) is at the heart of his problem. Thus an important operation can come to be the responsibility of a man who exists in a spiritual vacuum. It is not odd that at the crucial moment his compulsivity breaks down and he vanishes in an alcoholic haze.

It is not at all strange that the military has its problems. The ability to consume large quantities of alcohol and still function effectively has long been idealized as one of the tests of a man. In many of the civilizations that have marked the history of man, man has been put to the test of his ability to cope with excesses. Ultimately he flunks the test. In Greece and Rome, two civilizations basic to the western culture of today, excesses in food, drink, and sex, became the norm. In medieval times the drinking bout and the long, long days of feasting were the mark of power and importance. A real man had to handle excesses and still be able to stand on his own two legs and defend himself. Such a test was also the proof of virility in colonial America. As the American frontier was pushed westward, our culture moved backwards in time and its rules became more primitive. Whether a mountain man or a plainsman, the man of the West was expected to be able to drink, to brawl, and to come out alive. In the more effete East, the mark of a gentleman was to be able to hold his own with alcohol. Certainly the Southern man of means was marked by his ability to "hold his liquor."

All of this leads to the fact that the man of "business" today, as well as the military man, carries on in a long tradition. Today it is felt that a really effective operator must be able to match martini for martini (until he becomes like the man who had "tee many martunis") and come out ahead in negotiations for a contract. Indeed, if he cannot, he may lose out completely, for the people with whom he is negotiating will often envelop him in an "expense account" world of excesses, which will tend to lead him to part company with reality. As the world of business has tended more and more to include both husband and wife as a team, it is not strange that women have been subjected to the same problems. Many marriages have ended in divorce because of the inability of both husband and wife to cope with immoral excesses that have come to be accepted as "the thing to do."

Alcohol and the Military

It is hardly strange that such problems exist in the military as well as in industry. Indeed, the two seem to be growing closer and closer together. Defense contracts account for so large a part of our economy that business and the military were seen by a former president as the basis for an arrangement that could sink our democracy. It is interesting to note that a military man overseas finds himself surrounded by civilian technicians, or "tech-reps," also moved around the world by orders from those above them in the hierarchy of management. The civilian worker serving with the military tends to take on some of the color of his environment, and the chaplain finds that increasing amounts of his time are taken up in dealing with so-called "civilians."

Certainly the tradition of the soldier includes the right to act like an idiot (if he so chooses) on his free time. The military man is supposed to be able to drink as much as he wants when he is not on duty, and to report for duty no worse for wear. The social life of the officer is prescribed by both written and unwritten traditions. These traditions include the ability to drink like a "gentleman"—to "hold his likker." Most social functions, like their civilian counterparts, include the serving of alcohol, and the hostess who does not drink and who deplores the boorish behavior of those who do finds herself providing for the alcoholic refreshment of her guests. Indeed the commander, alarmed by the loss of efficiency of those who are bleary-eyed from the night before, nonetheless finds himself submitting to what appears to be a social dogma. Without alcohol, there is no salvation.

Add to the basic problem of the military the fact that many soldiers are quite immature and therefore are open to the leadership of those more experienced in the military milieu, and you have added some other complex problems. The young man of draft age is striving to become a "real man." His image of the "real man" is formed from his contacts with the more experienced. Hoping to be accepted as a rough and tough, take-on-all-comers type of a man, he is wide open for trouble. If in the barracks the senior men are brawlers and drinkers in their off-duty hours, the young man striving to identify with the truly virile will likely copy the failings of his idols, rather than those qualities which have made them successful in spite of their lack of standards. The young soldier is likely to feel his superiors are successful "because of" rather than "in spite of." Thus it is clear how important the non-commissioned leaders of a unit are, for they are the ones who live in the barracks with the new men. No matter what the commander does, no matter what the chaplain does, no matter what his mother or his wife writes, the young man is strongly tempted to experiment with excesses. What has been said has always been true of the age group concerned, wherever its members are living. If they are starting out in business, or enrolling in college, young people have always tended to make their mistakes in living during their teens and early twenties. Such is not to be approved, but it is a matter of human experience. Many effective, creative, sensitive people in their early years ran the danger of impairing their ability to produce. Many of us feel that we are simply lucky to have lived through our youthfulness without seriously damaging ourselves. The convert to the Church, whose emotional experience with religion gave him the power to break with bad habits of the past, makes this clear in his "testimonials." This is what led one man to ask why the saint, who has had his past, can't let the young person have his present?

However, it is fair to point out that this transitional period may be fraught with more perils in the military than in many civilian situations. The young man is far from home and is deprived of normal contacts with young women whom he thinks of as potential wives and mothers of his children. He has no need to appear to be responsible and worthy of trust. He is also often in an overseas area where alcohol and women are both readily available and inexpensive. His search for virility is not limited by the rules of his environment. He doesn't have to worry about Mrs. Grundy across the street. His mother, whom he may love, is faraway. His wife is not there to provide the solace of affection. Also, no one is there to take over the management of his funds. He can spend all of the cash he has on hand. Often he feels that any allotments he has ought to suffice for the home folks. *His* money is *his!* Didn't he earn it? Also, he finds that he does not lose face with his friends if he has to be dragged home a few nights. Each of his buddies works to keep the other out of the clutches of the military police. It is a fine, high-spirited game. In fact, he finds that an attempt to live a sensible life is often met with scorn from the guilt-ridden occupants of the same barracks. We can often bear physical pain much better than we can handle ridicule. It takes a mature man with a well-established inner system of controls to withstand a barrage of scorn.

Is it strange that the military chaplain has many puzzling problems involving heavy drinking and the more tragic problems arising out of it? The 20-year-old soldier who wants to marry the 30-year-old pregnant prostitute is well known to the military chaplain. How defensively the soldier proclaims that "This is real love." How emphatically he denies that guilt has anything to do with it. How sure he is that he simply couldn't have caused such a thing without being willing to accept responsibility for the outcome. Thus, when it is too late, the teachings of home and mother become ironically effective.

No, the strange thing is that so many young men do stand steadily against the temptations of their transient environment. The majority come through in fine shape. Those who fall are often put together too shakily to withstand even minimal temptations. They might have postponed their fall in the environs of home life, but they would probably have tumbled sooner or later. The military cannot accept the full blame for their failure. Indeed, it was the military that became convinced that young men and women were not receiving adequate training in basic morality in their homes, schools, or churches and thus began the training program identified as "Character Guidance." From subjects connected with battling the excesses of alcohol and sex activity, the program branched out to include questions of patriotism, the need for a high purpose in life, and so forth. Commanders were finding too much of their time taken up with problems that arose in off-duty time. Something *had* to be done. It is generally felt that the programs providing training in "how to live" have been helpful. However, it is still true that entirely too much time is taken up with those who fail. The costly time of commanders, doctors, social workers, chaplains, Red Cross workers, and others is devoted primarily to the small percentage of those who just cannot stand alone.

It is also ironic that the feeling the young person has that the rewards of the military go to the real, two-fisted, morally inadequate individual who is as "tough as they come" is exactly wrong. The military demands morally responsible leaders and followers. It demands stability and reliability. Trustworthiness is more valuable than genius in many military situations today. With the destructive potential in modern weaponry, it has become increasingly important to have men and women who can always be counted upon to act with common sense. In some highly critical areas of work, it is even necessary to report those men who feel the need to seek out the chaplain.

Such a need is not related to an attempt to break down the traditional privileged communication between minister and parishioner. Indeed, such a right has been more carefully spelled out in recent years. The need to know is based on the fact that some men are employed in such critical areas that even the fact that they have problems at all is important. Even if the problem is not of his making, it might be better to take him off of his present job until the problem is resolved. I repeat, in such areas of employment, stability and reliability are at a premium. The red-eyed and shaky individual may be a laughing matter on some jobs, but such is less and less the case in the military in our time.

The soldier who carouses is less and less desired by the military. In this respect commanders have become practical temperance workers. Many of our fine leaders spend hours struggling to find ways to keep their men out of the bars and away from the local immoral opportunists. In this respect the word of the chaplain is often sought. Only too often he has little to add to the commander's approach. When men are chronologically of age and have their rights within a democratic society, they have to be trusted to use their off-duty time wisely. To overcontrol is to invite a congressional investigation. The modern soldier is much quicker than was his predecessor to contact political figures with pen, pencil, or typewriter. The modern politician is, in many cases, just as sensitive as *his* predecessor to the need for votes. The military is not a voting bloc, but the home folks often do represent a real threat to a political career. Thus, the commander is on the horns of a three-pronged dilemma: He wants to have men on whom he can rely; he wants to be true to what he feels to be his obligation to the families at home; and he needs to do so without offending anyone. The three-pronged dilemma is, indeed, a most dangerous beast.

Basically, the problem sets up in this manner: A young soldier in the "age of rebellion" comes into an environment where on first glance it appears that excesses go with "soldiering"; he looks for leadership to those above him, but not so far above him that they are removed from his after-duty life. He sees people who live as he thinks he would like to and seemingly are rewarded for their pains. He copies the faults of his leaders rather than the qualities that have made them successful to this point. Then, he finds that he is in trouble because his commander cannot put up with instability, whatever the cause. The very environment that seemed to promise "free-dom" from basic morality, turns out to be an environment that de-mands uprightness of character. Thus, the permissive environment he thought he saw turns out to be a rigid, often punitive one.

Alcohol and the Career Man

Obviously, other problems arise. Few men can subject themselves to constant, heavy drinking through the years without drifting toward alcoholism. Inevitably they run into problems in their drink-ing, which earlier may not have bothered them. A typical problem is that of the soldier who served well in combat, continued to serve well in peace, and who finds that drink has taken him over. In com-bat he couldn't get much of it. When he did it was consumed in a brief binge and then he went back to duty where he couldn't in-dulge his habits. Earlier in his military career he could handle the stuff. But now, with several years of service and several more years added to his life, he finds that he is repeatedly late to work. Often he covers by requiring men under him to do his job, or by relying on friends of equal or higher rank to help him either by absorbing some of his responsibilities, or by adjusting their demands to his needs. Also he can keep himself from facing the problem by the time-honored methods of denial and projection. He has no problem. Peo-ple above him are simply unjust. After all, they drink, also. They owe him a little support when he has had a drop too much. The com-mander tries for a time to avoid dealing with the problem, but sooner or later he has to demand higher standards of the man. Complicating the problem is that, during all of this time he has been drifting into trouble, he has been accumulating a family. Now he has a wife and children to support and the military is his only profession. In many cases he does not have the training or the basic skills upon which he could rely outside of the military. To continue to take care of his family as their needs increase, he must work within the military. The commander weighs all of these matters and tries to find a way to help. He is embarrassed time and again by the failures of a key man. He sends the man to the chaplain. The results are what may be ex-pected. A man with alcohol problems cannot be helped until he admits the problem. He has been ordered to go, and the chaplain is thus identified with authority. Many chaplains try to avoid such interviews by keeping their commanders informed of the limitations of such "counseling." Others try to read the "riot act" to the man. Often the response is a variation of this comment actually made by a sergeant after he was "chewed out" by his chaplain: "I don't see why the Company Commander sent me to you—you are just like him."

Personally, I have tried to honor the desires of command, but at the same time have pointed out to the man that I know why he is before me and that I am sure he resents it. I thus encourage him to tell me his feelings, which I accept as valid under the circumstances. Then I give him the opportunity to tell me exactly how he does feel about all of this. Before we part, I point out that we have really not been in a counseling situation, but rather we have been carrying out a demand placed on both of us by a well-meaning authority figure. I then remind the man that he can come see me on his own in a relationship that is structured by the right of privileged communication. He is invited to come back on his own if he feels the need for help. Often I set up another appointment for about two weeks away, just as a chance to check on how things are going. In a few isolated cases this approach has worked and later has led to extended counseling and a tie-in with Alcoholics Anonymous. Frankly, in all too many cases the man simply does not come back, until he comes hoping to avoid or alleviate punishment that is pending for an act done when he was taken "unexpectedly and quite seriously drunk." Still I have found that such an approach has at least a chance of working, while others simply have not worked at all for me. (For detailed advice on work with the alcoholic and the problem drinker, see the companion volume by Tom Shipp in this series.)

Difficulties in Treatment

There are difficulties in working with such problems in the military. Traditionally, by its very reason for existence, the military has not wanted to look on itself as a reform school or treatment facility. Long-term, chronic problems such as drinking habits and emotional inadequacies have been outside of the scope of military medical facilities. Treatment has been made available in some instances by not admitting the primary cause of the trouble. Thus, by treating related matters such as physical disorders stemming from the alcohol problem, a compassionate medical officer might strive to help with the drinking problem. The military chaplain soon discovered such people and sought them out for assistance with men he knew about. But, by and large, the main approach has been to try to get the man out of the service as soon as possible without the need for a punitive discharge. The structure of regulations can be used in many instances to facilitate such a way of handling the problem.

A chaplain, in working with the many tragic cases which are always in his ken, struggles in a net. He wants to help. He wants the man to be able to stay within his chosen profession and enjoy the benefits of retirement. He wants to avoid punitive action on the part of command, and yet he appreciates the basic mission of the Army and the problems of the commander. He knows also that often, if he tries to keep the man going by manipulative techniques and by alternating pleas and threats, he will only keep the man in the thick of the problem. Thus the chaplain has increased the possibility that the individual will fail at a crucial moment and bring down the heavy weight of punishment upon himself. Also, where the man is on a critical job, the chaplain must not attempt to keep the problem hidden, since eventually the lives of many could be hurt by a moment of failure. Often the commander and the chaplain work together to hide the problem and keep the man going at least until he transfers out of the organization. It is now felt, and a recent study of the matter underlines this fact, that such attempts to keep a man going from day to day without facing the problem directly may be responsible for allowing the matter to deteriorate beyond help. In such cases the approach has been about as helpful as trying to keep a man with cancer away from significant treatment until it is too late. However, the study referred to raises some problems by the solution it appears to offer. The solution was one of milieu therapy (treatment by the total environment) combining group techniques and one-to-one techniques with trained psychotherapists and also with nurses, ward employees, and other individual sufferers. Such treatment, while admittedly sounding valuable, would apparently put more strain on the military environment than it can afford. Again the question comes, "Is the military designed for long-term treatment of any disorder?" Perhaps other government agencies ought to be developed to take over, and a method worked out by which a man with many years of good service might be placed on an administrative leave of absence for treatment, with a possibility of being returned to duty to complete his years for retirement if the treatment is effective. Thus, during the period of treatment the military would not be charged with the body, nor would the man be constantly subject to the punishment which failures in the military demand. Whether or not as a tax-burdened nation we can afford such a recommendation is beyond the scope of this book.

Alcohol and the Military Wife

The burden of these comments has been directed toward the military individual. Obviously his family is involved, as with all drinking problems. In another way the military wife is often involved. She, too, when she is with her husband, lives within the environment. Socially, the pressure toward drinking is as heavy as it is within some large corporations in our day. The husband feels the need to drink or to serve drinks in the house. The wife goes along with the pressure. She must make sure that her man's career is advanced. Perhaps the wives take up the pattern of drinking as a matter of course in social gatherings. Their women's groups may make certain that cocktails or at least wines are available for luncheons and teas. The wife may find her husband sent away on orders for months at a time. In her boredom she may find solace in heavy drinking and before long she may become sexually careless and find her life even more confused. These problems are not only those of the military wife in our transient culture, but it is clear that the military wife is not free from the threat of alcoholism, compulsive drinking, or related problems.

Implications for the Civilian Pastor

The civilian pastor may meet the problem of alcohol and the military family in several ways. It may be that the wife, still at home and striving to take care of the family in the husband's absence, feels a financial pinch and begins to be aware something is wrong. It may be that she hears that her husband has been reduced in grade due to an alcoholic escapade, and now she knows she must adjust to a lower standard of living for a long time. It may be that his drinking leads to marital infidelity of which she becomes aware. In these cases, the pastor's task would be to help her with her feelings about her husband, and perhaps to get her some help in working out a budget, or in some other way to help her understand herself and her situation. Perhaps, when it is evident that the problem is one of alcohol, the pastor might help the wife read all she can on the matter, and also refer her to Al-Anon where she might meet with others who are living with the same problem.

In facing such problems involving service families a civilian pastor may be called upon to assist a man discharged for problems which may be related to drinking patterns to understand his need for help and to encourage him to seek it. During the period of adjustment the pastor can provide counseling and may offer the support of the community in obtaining work to enable the husband to support his family as he strives to adjust to civilian life. The material in this chapter is offered to assist the civilian pastor without military experience to understand how such problems develop within the military environment. Perhaps such an understanding will make his work with the family or with the returned serviceman more effective.

It has been observed in other writings that the best thing the Church can offer in problems of alcohol, drugs, compulsive gambling, and other related matters is a sense of purpose in life that transcends self. To proclaim a way of life that is stronger than frustration, more powerful than the worst that life can face us with, and more rewarding than any form of self-indulgence is to provide a man with a sense of meaning that overcomes the meaninglessness which besets anyone who tries to make his way in life without God. Thus it is important that clergymen, whether military or civilian, do their best to assist their people to provide a Church that sees itself as a redemptive community in a troubled world, rather than as a punitive community in a sinful one. The clergyman who can lead his people to such a relationship with God that they can find a sense of meaning capable of filling the spiritual vacuum (which all too often is the lot of man in this materialistic, sensate culture) has served a purpose that is invaluable. He must also develop his counseling skill; he must know all he can about the problems of this world. He must strive to provide groups within his Church to minister to all sorts

of troubled people. He must do all these things, but he must not
forget that the greatest therapy is God's forgiving love and His willingness to share His work of redemption with those who are most
in need of being redeemed. No other meaning is greater than that
found in co-operating with God in His work of leading His children
into a community of love that transcends even life itself.

CHAPTER SEVEN

"If I COULD ONLY GET PROMOTED!"
(*Financial Problems and the Military*)

"If I could only get promoted, I know I could make it," the young man said emphatically. The chaplain could not help but think of other men and women, young and not so young, who had made the same statement through the years. He could not help but think of his own life, as he moved from one pay grade to the next, wondering each time where all the money went. How easy it is to adjust to a higher pay scale! How co-operative is our culture in assisting us always to live a little beyond that which we can afford. The old song goes, "For I always have afforded anything that I could get," and that is certainly true of many of us in our world of today.

The fact is that the statement *is* partially true. At many military pay levels the going is pretty tough. Promotions are slow and families tend to grow. The needs of the children seem to increase by geometrical progression. The demands for school clothing, materials, and luxuries that are important (if the children are not to feel like "oddballs" compared with their friends) all combine to strain already weakening budgets. Sometimes the only apparent answer is to get more money. It is difficult in the military to hold outside jobs. First, military demands on a man's time cannot be limited to a clear-cut eight-hour day with week ends all or partially off. Secondly, because of this, outside jobs must be approved by the commander for several reasons. The job must not be too demanding on a man's time, and it certainly must not be one which might embarrass the military. Such necessary limitations make it difficult for a man to get a job, for the employer must agree that the job will be a part-time affair, allowing full precedence for the demands of the military on the man. Aside from alerts and special training demands taking a man from his post for anywhere from a few days to several weeks, there are other necessary administrative limitations.

Sometimes it is possible for the wife to get a job. But in the families where money is needed, it is often just as important for the wife to be at home with the children. Even in some foreign stations where inexpensive domestic help can be obtained, it is often considered less than the best thing to do to leave the younger children in the hands of the maids. Many times the maids are open-hearted toward little children and are willing to devote their time to them, but this may lead to the creation of a new problem, for a spoiled child in any setting is a difficult one. Then, too, the location of military bases may limit the number of civilian jobs possible. The demand for workers may be limited to special skills or to such unskilled work that the pay connected with it helps only in a token way. Sometimes the work can be done just as efficiently at less cost by the natives of the region, so that it is uneconomical to hire Americans for the task.

Certainly the enlisted grades suffer. Recently in some American communities enlisted men and their families have been found to be eligible for assistance from welfare groups. The scale applied has compared their wage scales and their needs with other groups of the local citizenry and has come up with the answer that they need help. Perhaps it is true that in many cases these people would have faced the same problem had they tried to make a living in a civilian world. Yet, in some cases, these individuals are well trained and simply want to work within the military. These potentially fine military men may have to drop out of the service against their wishes in order to take care of their families. Since career men in the higher enlisted grades are the backbone of the military, whatever the branch, it is evident that we are dealing with a danger area. With promotion slow and pay limited in the lower grades, how can a potentially valuable enlisted man be retained long enough to begin to get a true return on his experience? In the old days it was true that the lower grades were made up of young, single males, with a minimum of financial demand upon them. But today more and more young people are marrying in their late "teens," if the warnings of sociologists and the writers of magazine articles are to be trusted, and the financial needs take a quick bounce toward the heights. Recent pay raises are gestures in the right direction, but often their best help does not go to the man in the pay grades we are considering. Compared to the raises of civilians, both in and out of government service, the military pay raises are too few and too slight. Perhaps the fact that the military is not a significant voting bloc has some application here. Whatever the solution, the problem is a very real one.

Working hand-in-glove with the realistic situation described is a fine, old military tradition. The soldier pays his debts! He does not allow his handling of his finances to become an embarrassment to the service. It may be that this tradition has been often honored more in the breach, yet it remains a strong factor in the thinking of any military commander. Often the troop commander down the line is sympathetic with the problems his men face, if only because in some ways they are very similar to his own, but the pressure comes from up the line. This is not to say that it should be otherwise; this is simply to look at the problem as it exists. The senior commander cannot afford to have letters of indebtedness flocking into his command. His career hinges often on just such matters. Also he is sincerely committed to the fact that the military man ought to be beyond reproach. Since he has been able to get through his earlier career without getting beyond his depth (even though it may have been touch and go at one time or another), he is inclined to be fairly rigid in his demands on those beneath him. This he must be, if he is to help his men develop as they should, but it does put the pinch on many. So the problem develops inexorably. Pay scales, the demands of family life, slow promotions, easy credit, and the tradition that the military pays its debts inevitably lead to trouble for many.

Special Financial Demands
Related to the Military Life

In the distant past it was considered in other countries, as well as our own, that a military career was to be sought only by those who had independent means. The lower grades were so far down the scale in their culture anyway that their needs were not to be considered. Many of them were in the military to get out of going to jail, to run from an unfortunate marital venture, or due to an irresponsible love of adventure. They were the fringe groups of society anyway. Those in the mainstream of life could allow themselves a military career only if they were already well off. There are days when I wonder if such is not the case today. There are periods of time when almost all military families are forced to borrow or to cash bonds, or otherwise to deplete their savings.

When orders come to move, the military family has no choice. Often the serviceman cannot even get out of the service by retiring or by resigning. There may be no government quarters available at the new station or the family may face a long, expensive wait for on-post housing. If the husband is assigned to a hardship tour where the family cannot accompany him, he must quickly find somewhere to move them. Usually this means that he is in a poor situation to bargain. He often must accept substandard housing at luxury costs. The move must be accomplished quickly. And it is often final for the duration of his hardship tour. The government will move his household goods but will not repeat such a task without specific regulations to back it up. Thus the move is made, the family is "closed-in" for better or for worse and must settle back to tough it out until its members can be together again.

Although the government handles a great proportion of the expense, that remaining proportion is not a simple matter to the family involved. The old saying used to be "Three moves equal one fire." There are many military families who will tell you, "*One* move does the trick." Always there are added expenses in the temporary stages. The family moves, first storing its goods near the base or sending them ahead to be stored in the area where they hope to live. Its home, like the Joad family's, must be the car. With the vehicle loaded down, with a carrier on top, with the children crowded into the back seat, the family takes off. Mother must either pack plenty of auxiliary cooking equipment, or the family must live the expensive way. There is no way to feed a family adequately while on the road without running into more expense than would be true in a settled situation. The trip itself may involve many miles. The expenses of the trip, including gasoline, repairs, the purchase of new tires, and so forth are always considerable. Add to the financial problems the anxious moments as to where to live, however to get together again, what will happen to the family, and you have a great deal of tension.

Assume a fairly uneventful trip, and then consider other problems. If the family has no relatives with whom they can live a parasitical existence for a short time, they must either camp out (which requires expensive equipment itself, plus added charges for a camping space, water, and electricity) or live a gypsy-like life in motor courts or other temporary (and expensive) facilities.

Then comes the problem of getting into a home quickly enough to get the children into school. The family is under pressure and "papa's" time is running out. He must move on to his next assignment. He may have to leave with the problem yet unsolved and the welfare of his family heavily on his mind. Also during the interim period many purchases must be made. Some things are too heavy or too unwieldy to pack and move, but they are necessary for the family to keep going. So duplicate purchases are often made of items that are in storage awaiting a more permanent address. Add to this the problem of laundry without the family washing machine, and the difficulty of preparing meals in makeshift quarters, and you can see how financial demands would tend to multiply.

If these problems are solved and the family is left in a fairly secure situation, there are yet other difficulties that have financial, as well as emotional, implications. Papa goes faraway and is assigned bachelor quarters in a distant land. At home, his needs could be met along with the family's without stepping up expenses greatly. Away from home he becomes an added financial drag. Even with bachelor quarters furnished, there are expenses which add to the total burden of the family. If he is to live at all comfortably, he will have to make purchases which will complicate the family budget. He must eat, be clothed, have some means of transportation (a fact that is increasingly true because our military establishments are no longer posts in the old sense of a rather compact area but instead sprawl for many miles over the countryside), and, if he is not to go absolutely berserk, he does have some need for entertainment. The need for relaxation and wholesome entertainment becomes even greater, for he does not have evenings with his family to restore him after a full day of military demands. Even a very careful, rather undemanding person, will have certain financial demands that will require more funds than would be needed if the family were together.

Away from home, he may be in an area where government housing is limited, but he is allowed to bring his family over to occupy "approved" private rentals on the civilian economy. Here he finds that rental prices always expand to more than match his rental allowance. This is as inexorable as the law of gravity. No matter what the limitations of the housing he must occupy, the rent will match the funds he is provided for such living. Then, in addition to the rent, come the necessary bills for water and electrical power. The family is trying to recover from a move across America to another area, a period of separation when father must go it alone, and another move across country to a port of embarkation. Their recovery must be worked out while facing added expenses of off-post living, wherever they are. The civilian pastor may ask, "Why don't the families accept the long time of separation as 'one of those things' and simply 'tough it out'?" However, if he recalls seriously the counseling that he has had to do with separated families, he will find his own answer. It is not a healthy thing for families to be separated for a long period of time. Where it is absolutely necessary, it can be done. When it is possible to be together, even with difficulty, families ought to be together. Young children need both parents. They tend unconsciously to equate father's absence with deliberate desertion. "Father has gone. There must be a reason. He doesn't like us. I must have caused this dislike, since, as 'father' he would not be unfair." And a real problem develops, often expressing itself in later years as a difficulty for the child in getting along with authority figures, or an inordinant fear of separations from loved ones, even when necessary. It may be recalled that since "There are more people married in this world than are doing well at it," any added tensions can plunge a marital relationship into stormy seas of trouble. For these, and many other reasons, the pastor will recognize that families ought to be together no matter what the financial difficulties.

It ought also to be recognized that those very financial difficulties can also threaten the relationship. Let the husband overseas keep more of the family funds for his living than the wife thinks he should have—and there is trouble. Or perhaps he feels that the allotment his wife receives ought to be quite adequate, but she finds that demands are greater than they had expected. Her letters asking for more help may be based on sound common sense and a realistic appraisal of the situation, but to him they ring the alarm bell of feminine financial irresponsibility. The chaplain overseas and the pastor at home will find their abilities taxed in helping the families to cope with such misunderstandings. In such instances, it is important that the clergymen involved avoid overidentification with the persons they are seeing. A compassionate hearing can be offered without falling into the trap of emotional involvement beyond the bounds of common sense. The problem is real because the pastor at home understands the financial demands of the community, while the overseas chaplain sees the matter as colored by his own problems and desires. Remembering the chapter dealing with the problems of communication in such matters, the pastor and the chaplain would do well to move carefully to enhance the feeling of oneness, rather than to accentuate the differences.

Added Financial Problems for the Emotionally Immature

So far, we have looked at financial problems that are a natural part of military life. No matter how intellectually and emotionally adequate the individuals concerned are, these problems have to be faced. As family emergencies (accidents, serious illnesses, and so on) are mixed in the same pot, even the strongest can find themselves in over their heads. As it is necessary to borrow or to draw on emergency financial cushions, these problems become even more threatening. But let's leave the normal, natural problems of life and move into the realm of added problems caused by the characterological structure of the persons concerned, as complicated by the irresponsible attitudes of the mind-set of our times.

We definitely live in a "thing" world. We have shown our ability to produce "things" that promise an easier or more exciting life for us. Other nations want to copy us. They would like to sell to us on such a basis that their ability to acquire things such as those we have is increased. This is understandable. Since, in most cases, the people of these nations have not had our "good" fortune, their labor is cheap and the things they produce can be offered at a very low price. Often the heavy burden of taxation is not involved and the prices can stay down. With prices low, who can pass up the "bargains"? It may be true that a thing is never a bargain unless it is needed, but this is a truth beyond the understanding of most of us. A thing can be a bargain even if we must plunge ourselves into debt to "afford" it. Let a serviceman see an item that he knows would cost $500.00 in America, but can be obtained for only $379.00 where he is, and he has got to have it. His wife may often second him in that decision, unless she has found a bargain that she wants even more. The matter is often resolved by buying both items.

In our culture we are likely to equate our individual worth with what we have. "What is he worth?" we say, and we mean, "How much does he own?" Often what we own has only a slight relation to how much cash we have on hand or in the bank, but that is beside the point. A man is as good as his car, his stereophonic equipment, and his fishing and hunting accessories. A woman is as good as her clothing, her jewelry, and the other appointments of her home. We are also a nation of strong competitors. Thus a new problem appears. Certainly we are as good as the Joneses. So we have to keep ahead of them—not up with them, but ahead of them. Put an American family down in the midst of other American families, all gleefully acquiring "bargains," and an invisible, but nonetheless real, pressure is created. Sometimes the urge to compete appears as "co-operation" in such matters. Thus one wife who finds an area where there are real bargains will quickly tell others. She gets points for having found it first. The others must not let her stay ahead, and away they go! In the meantime the husband, thrown into contact with the community during his work or perhaps advised by some civilian worker from the local population, is discovering his own bargains. In his case the problem may be aggravated by his being sent away for short periods of time on duty to nearby areas where the bargains are even greater. He may leave on a tour of duty with a list from his wife, plus the authority from her to buy up anything else which he sees to be a real buy.

Add to all of this the upsurge of "easy" credit in any community bordering on or containing a military establishment. The credit offered adjusts itself to the desires of all ranks. Knowing the threat to an officer's career if he does not pay up, banks are quick to offer loans to commissioned personnel. With a recent thrust in the direction of real punitive action toward a non-commissioned officer who fails to pay, civilian establishments are increasingly willing to do large-scale business with them. More and more loan companies and other financial institutions send their invitations out to a mailing list compiled from military sources.

For those who, in lower pay brackets, may have desires that are proportionately greater than their income, we have the "pawnshop" alleys that spring up like poisonous toadstools in the night. Here the soldier, sailor, or airman may not only find great "buys" on which to spend money beyond his means but here, when he can't pay for what he has, he can sell other items which he is more prepared to do without, and thus make up enough cash for another "easy" payment. The fact that these establishments inevitably offer encouragement to petty thievery must not be discounted, either, but that is another story.

Multiplying like hamsters in any community related to the military, are the short-term loan establishments operating just within the law in most cases, and probably just without it in others. Here the serviceman is told he can consolidate his debts and pay only one amount. The fact that such a move has only added to his total indebtedness is ignored. The readiness of all of these establishments to make such ventures is based on the high proportion of profit they make on those who can pay up. They also work with the knowledge that the unit commander will have to help them if they hound the man with letters of indebtedness. He may loudly insist, "I am not a collection agency," but what he must do speaks louder than what he says. He knows that he cannot afford to have such letters flocking in down through the chain of command. His senior commanders will not tolerate it. His career will be hurt if he does not take action to correct the situation and get the civilian agency off the back of the military. In some cases he must make sure that his action against his men, who are in over their heads, is stringent enough to reassure his seniors that he is serious about this. The chaplain and the unit commander tend to find an unhealthy proportion of their time is taken up in counseling or advising servicemen on financial matters. The action taken will in some cases involve a reduction in grade and thus decrease the amount of money available to pay off past debts. Since a reduction under the present system of promotion means a long hard haul to get back to where you were, the punishment is quite long lasting. In some cases really competent men are forced to get out of the service to recoup their losses. Many of these problems occur while the men are quite young and cannot be expected to have the maturity necessary for living in the financial jungle in which they find themselves. If a pathway could be hacked through the undergrowth of "easy" credit out into the clearer path of experience and maturity, some of these men might make it the rest of the way in good order.

Making the matter even more complex is the modern knowledge of advertising psychology. Such knowledge may not even be conscious knowledge, but is the result of observing with the shrewdness of greed what the facts of experience add up to. Make your advertising pitch in the direction of overcoming a man's feeling of insecurity, and eventually you will make sales. Imply that his worth in the eyes of his friends will be built up by the product on sale, and you are in business. Add to this the heavy-handed implication that his sexual attractiveness will be increased if he buys this particular gadget, and you have set another trap. Make him feel that his virility, his desirability, and his power over others will be increased by whatever it is, be it automobile or electric shaver, and you will either get *him* some other day or another one like him that very day.

Perhaps the serviceman concerned is actually pretty level-headed. He has a certain amount of security which has been with him since his childhood, placed there by the real love his parents had for him. He has a certain amount of experience and has learned to use his head to avoid trouble. He is not basically very greedy, although he does like to live as well as he can within his means. Say he is happily married to a woman of good common sense and feels a true sense of responsibility toward her and the children, if there are any. Even take this paragon, and someday you might "hook" him. He is a good one to "hook," for he will work like mad to pay up and stay out of trouble. How does he become susceptible? It is simple. Most of the time there is no danger. He passes easily by attractive advertisements about things he would really like to have. He does not succumb to the "nothing down" inducements, for he knows those forty-eight "easy" installments are actually backbreaking obligations. But then comes the time when possibly he's had a misunderstanding with his wife over the children, or she has been worn out and unable to offer the affection upon which he often relies; anyway, for one reason or another he does not feel as "wanted" as he usually does. Maybe he has thought over his career chances and is a bit downhearted. He has reached a stage in life when the question of "What's ahead for me?" is much more important than it once was. Add to this a rebuke from his boss for a job that was not quite up to standard, and you see the problem. This day of all days the same "deal" he has by-passed many times without difficulty will ensnare him. It takes only a few seconds to get a name down on an order blank, but it may take months to complete the final payments. A few moments of despondency can end in long months of financial annoyance, to say the least. The point is that the appeal does not let up. The man does. Immersed in an environment that promises its blessings in terms of things possessed, the struggle against temptation never ends.

Since most of us are not as worthy as the "paragon" described above, it is not strange that financial trouble abounds. It should be apparent that many "financial" troubles are actually personality conflicts. Finances can be used as an aggressive move against a marriage partner. They can be used to get even with a spouse. They can be used to compensate for feelings of insecurity. An unimportant man feels big behind the wheel of a flashy new car, even if it belongs to the finance company. A man who is not fully adequate on the job may feel ten feet tall when he is showing off an expensive stereophonic set he was able to put together in off-duty time. A sexually inadequate male may feel like a "white giant" when he presents his girl with an expensive diamond. Didn't the advertisement tell him that she would fall into his arms when he presented it? Money is a projection of personality and is so used. If that personality is fairly well put together there are problems enough, for no one is perfect. If that personality is a flimsy shell of a structure, then there is real trouble. From this group of the poorly constructed come the compulsive gamblers who cannot pass up a game of cards, a dice table, or a "one-armed bandit." Like alcoholics they are sick, and yet it is difficult to treat them as worthy of assistance. Their illness robs their children of food and clothing and creates headaches for all who touch them. A small loan to help a gambler, turns out to be only an invitation to greater disaster. It has been said that at least twenty people are seriously affected by each alcoholic, and it would certainly be as easy to believe that an equal number are hurt by each compulsive gambler.

What to Do about It?

The military establishment actually has, either within itself or associated with it, several fine resources for the man in trouble. It is recognized that most of us live so close to the border that a rash of trouble can put us over the brink financially. In some instances the American Red Cross can be of tremendous help either to the man overseas or to the family at home through the local Red Cross office. Emergency relief is available through organizations that have grown up strictly as attempts of the military to help its own. Often in addition to possibilities for emergency assistance, there are organizations, such as credit unions, existing to make loans to military personnel. Such groups are certainly to be remembered when one is striving to assist a man in trouble. However, it is easy to make the mistake of assuming that financial problems can be solved by a practical method of adding up the expenses and comparing them with the income and the actual needs, then setting up a system of payments to keep the creditors off of a man's back. This kind of bookkeeping does not require a professionally competent clergyman. The pastor or chaplain who approaches financial problems from such a viewpoint is often one who unconsciously doubts the importance of his profession. If he is giving good, clear advice on how to handle practical problems, he can feel important. His own inadequacies within his role are less painfully obvious while he is adding up columns of figures. However, he has forgotten that man is not a creature of intellect alone; man has moral and emotional attributes that are basic to his nature, and that usually dominate the merely intellectual. He does not discount the intellect, but he realizes that it can function best only when emotional problems are dealt with to the point where tension is at least slight enough to allow clear judgment to operate. The clergyman deals with the basic man and not with surface attributes, if he is true to his calling.

The real problem for the counselor is to establish a relationship which will enable the individual to understand the battleground his attitudes and feelings are providing for his financial "problems." Like sex, finances are expressions of personality that are best dealt with by assisting the person to grow toward an ability to sustain a mature relationship with another. Until a person has a healthy attitude toward God and man, he will be unable to avoid problems of relationship. Problems of relationship are invariably expressed in symptomatic ways. To work only on the symptom is to overlook the basic cause. To handle a man's persistently recurring financial problems, without assisting him to develop a sense of purpose and a deep sense of responsibility toward others, is like attempting to put out a forest fire by stamping on the sparks.

The answer that really answers in the matter of financial problems, as with other problems, must inevitably involve the total man. Such a solution will not be found only by reading oversimplified "How to" handbooks, although they can sometimes be helpful if used with common sense. The real answer is only to be found by long-term training in counseling procedures, formal and informal, supervised and alone. Such training in reality may be said to take place throughout an entire career. It is never finally completed. The answer involves the constantly growing ability of the counselor to assist others in the direction of growth. Once this point of view is understood and accepted, the chaplain, and the civilian pastor as well, is likely to be increasingly helpful to those who seek his services.

CHAPTER EIGHT

"I DIDN'T KNOW It WOULD Be LIKE THIS"

(Preparing Youth for Military Life)

"But they told me I could go to school. I asked for training in electronics, but all I'm doing is pushing papers in the orderly room and going on any kind of lousy detail they think of. I just didn't know it would be like this! If I had, I sure would have made them draft me. They would have had to come and get me, I can tell you that!"

The young man had come to get the chaplain to see why he was not getting the training the recruiter had promised him or, at least, that he *thought* the recruiter had promised him. The chaplain, of course, knew that the problem was one that would be handled only through personnel channels. He knew whom to call to find out the exact status of the young man's chances for the training he wanted. But he also knew something else—the need the young man had for someone who would listen. The importance of being there to respond to feelings and to provide emotional support for the inner struggle the young man was undergoing was clear to this chaplain, as it would be to most.

Only a part of the problem was caused by a conflict between what the recruiter actually said and what the young man wanted to hear. Only partly was it caused by a failure of the recruited to read carefully the papers that were signed. The chaplain knew that even the best recruiter is naturally trying to make a sale. He wants to be truthful, because he has to continue to live in the community, but he certainly doesn't want to present the military service in less than the best light. The recruiter wants to do a good job and keep his assignment. All of this is natural. On the other side of the picture, the young civilian does not have the experience he needs to listen carefully for possible areas of misunderstanding. He needs to know the proper questions to ask and how to phrase them precisely, but this he can learn only through experience. All of these facts tend to set up later problems, it is true. But they do not tell the whole story.

Complicating the matter is the great amount of fantasy that tends to cluster around an organization such as the military, whether it be the Army, Navy, Marines, or the Air Force. As is the case of the Church and the medical profession, the military carries with it an aura of mystical meaning. Unconscious fears and wishes alike are stirred into action. Inner problems may help draw the young person, as does a magnet, into a net. As his mistakes are recognized, all too often he begins to react with panic, and the resulting struggle only ties him more closely to his problem.

The military, like the Foreign Legion, offers a way out of troubles. And never doubt the terrific emotional torment that goes with adolescence and the agonizing struggle toward maturity! Erik Ericson has probably written as effectively as anyone on this conflict, which he calls "ego identity versus role diffusion." By this he means partly that young people go through a stage in their development where they must ask the question, "Who am I?" They do this by searching about for a role they'd like to fit. Thus they look to the gang, to the friends they have in school, to the opportunities offered them by the environment. They try themselves out as "the athlete," as "the bookworm," as the "social lion," as the deeply religious "man of faith." Thus it is not strange that parents have difficulty in understanding their teen-agers. Which teen-ager are they to understand? The great lover? The hard-hitting, tough football player? The sensitive artist? The black-jacketed gang leader? And since the parents may be having role troubles of their own, it is not strange that there are problems at home.

The time comes in the lives of many when any resolution of the problem is better than the chaos that exists. One man cried out that there was enough chaos in him to create a whole new universe. Indeed, the only way out of chaos may be the unconscious creation of a new universe, or dream world. Thus, the young man who is troubled with doubts as to his ability to assume the male role, to be fully masculine, may create in his mind a way out of the problem. He may strive to identify closely with the military and thus become a man. In the military certainly all of his doubts will be put to sleep. His weaknesses, he feels, will be obliterated, his strong points accentuated, and he will be a real man.

Not all men are like the man who joined the Foreign Legion to forget, and on the day he signed up, he forgot what it was he had wanted to forget. All the years stretched ahead of him, now devoid of their purpose. Yet many come close to this same fate. They enter the military service, hoping to grow up. Then, they do grow up, and they find that life's answers are not so easily obtained. They find that they must continue to work with their inner problems and that the willingness to accept this fact is part of growth. They see that their questions are not going to be put to sleep by their identification with a cosmic authority figure. Seeing this, they no longer see the need for such a life. Yet the terms of their contracts hold them for several years beyond their disillusionment.

Others join and so overdo the identification bit that they become problems for the organization with which they are trying to identify. They swagger about, talking loudly and playing the role of the tough soldier. They copy the mistakes of older soldiers, rather than their good points. Inevitably they are drawn toward a clash with the realistic demands of the military. Their soldiering is not what the military wants from them. In fact, as they think they become real men, they become less than the man the military has to have.

The extreme case of the basic problem that draws the man deeper into the net of his personal problems, is that of the latent homosexual. He is struggling against an unconscious fear that he can never be a man. To overcome such a fear, he wants so to identify with "father" that there is no mistake. Suffering from a lacerated unconscious mind, he wants to apply the poultice of the military. He will become all man. He will be a soldier, or a sailor, or a marine. He does not realize that his solution to the problem that besets him will actually only aggravate it. In the barracks, or on shipboard, his fears are stirred into activity. His mind gives him no rest. And he knows that if his fears materialize, he will be punished by the "father" he wanted so much to please. Seeking an answer to his problem, he has only compounded it. But for most, the problem is certainly not so extreme. It is primarily only in search of an answer to the basic question of "Who am I?" that the young man seeks out a military career. He wants to grow up; he wants to do away with the welter of confusion that rules him in his adolescent years, and the military seems to offer the true answer.

Actually he does not have the facts he needs to justify such a conclusion. Later he can be quite sincere when he says, "I didn't know it would be like this!" The knowledge he thought he had, he had gained from overly sentimentalized moving pictures, or novels, or television shows that seemed to be realistic yet were not. Chance conversations he has had with adults who have seen military life at first-hand are colored by their desire to remember only the best part of their lives in the service. Even the rough times they remember as most amusing. Others who "help" them may be friends who did enlist and who don't wish their mistake to be known. At home on leave it is a good feeling to let people see you as a happy, roving adventurer. From these and other similar sources the young man draws his "facts." Then, if he does not wait to be drafted, he talks to a recruiter whose own place in life may make it difficult for him to overcome the young man's mistaken impressions. He doesn't want the military life to look bad. He wants to be truthful, but his truth is often colored in such a way as to blend with the young man's desires to create a life that never was.

How the Church Might Help

As a pastor reads this, he may see a similarity between the problem of the young man and the military service, and other problems for which he strives to prepare his people. He knows, for instance, that the sexual attitudes his young people have are formed by a meeting of unconscious drives with a conspiracy of society to conceal the necessary facts for coping with a natural problem. He knows that the young (and the old, for that matter) get answers to their questions about their sex life from the unqualified. The pastor knows the young man and woman find answers to such questions from other inexperienced, immature, troubled people. He knows that the dirty joke plus the overly romanticized attitude toward the sex act itself combine to confuse the issue. He knows that the modern "case-history" novel, often written by either disturbed people or those who callously strive to cash in on the financial appeal of the bizarre, is only too available. He knows also that the frustrated adult, who is obviously horrified by the existence of such questions in the minds of the young, only confuses the matter in another direction. He finds that the school often is unable to provide proper instruction, either from a lack of desire or from a negative climate of public opinion.

He finds that parents who have never worked out their own sex problems are too threatened by the questions of the young to be able to handle them sensibly. He spends much of his time counseling the married couples in his community, who are in difficulty because of their lack of preparation for the physical side of marriage, and he knows of the need for sex education in the Church. He sees also that the medical profession has neither the time nor the inclination to enter into the field of preliminary sex education, and he sees that the task must be assumed by the Church. Add to this the tragic cases he has in mind where young people have been unable to cope with their drives, and he knows he must provide some opportunity for the young to get "the facts of life." The cynicism and phony sophistication of the young only tend to hide their basic insecurity and abysmal ignorance. They know the words, but they never heard the melody.

So the local church works with educators, psychologists, medical doctors, and trained laymen to set up programs of lectures, group discussions involving the young people and trained adults, group work with both parents and the young, films, guided reading, and individual personal conferences—all pointed toward the end result of a young person better prepared to meet the demands of a real world.

It seems to me that a similar chain of thought should lead to the setting up of a training program within the local parish to provide preliminary instruction in the nature of the military life. Since we are still living in a world where military service is compulsory for many and where, even without legal compulsion, the temper of the times stresses the importance of military strength, the local church ought to feel the need to help the young of the parish toward a realistic understanding of the military. As churches provide training for the young, for those about to be married, for those about to select a vocation, for those about to become parents, for those facing retirement, and for many others who must face the demands that this life inexorably thrusts upon us, so should they provide training for the life of the military serviceman.

Resources within the Parish

Where can the church find qualified people for a program of training? In many cases we can start with the pastor himself. Often the pastor has spent time in the military service before he went to the seminary. He may have served as an enlisted man, or he may have gone into the military from the ROTC program and have served as an officer. He may even have served as a chaplain. At any rate, often the pastor has enough knowledge to qualify him to set up such a program. Even if his own experiential reaction to the military has been negative, he should at least see the necessity for such service. If he cannot see the necessity, he must see that whether he believes it to be necessary or not, the demands of his Government will insure a taste of the military life for many of his church's young people.

If the pastor has had military experience, he will immediately think of others who could be helpful in training his young people for a period of military service. He will think of men (and women) in his church who have been in the service. He will think of retired service people in the community. He will remember to go to nearby colleges to talk to ROTC advisors, who are often people carefully selected for the effective job they can perform with young, intellectually curious individuals. He will remember that the reserve units in his area, with which some of his parishioners are drilling, have advisors assigned to assist them. Certainly he will seek out these active duty people and enlist their help. Again, they are selected for their sensitivity to the attitudes of the civilian community and thus are well suited for an active part in a program such as the one envisioned.

The pastor, convinced of the necessity for an opportunity for his young people to learn as much as possible about the demands of a military life before they are propelled into it, will visit nearby military posts and confer not only with the post or base chaplains, but also with the commanders. These men are busy, but they are only too aware of the need for such a training program. Too much of their time is taken up working with the problems of those unprepared for military life for them to be unsympathetic to a local pastor embarked on such a project of education. The pastor will likely find them to be immediately active in assisting him with his program. Such people can provide leaders for discussion groups, qualified lecturers on various aspects of military life, opportunities for visits to the military installation to observe servicemen in action, and other aids toward understanding the advantages and disadvantages of a life in the military. The post chaplain might even set up discussion groups with servicemen and women who attend the chapel services and work with the military church school, and those of the local church who are enrolled in the training program. Such classes would assist the young person in the local church to understand the opportunities and the problems that confront the religious person in the military. Most commanders would welcome such opportunities to be of service to the community, for their task is made easier in direct proportion to the amount of understanding in the local community about the military. He also knows that his people can learn from the civilians in the program much about community problems and attitudes which will assist him in his role as the commander of a nearby military installation. After all, many of his people are also citizens of the local community. Some of his people might be active in the very church involved. No pastor need be apologetic as he explores the possibilities for assistance from military units. In many instances they will provide his most effective instructors.

The pastor should also remember the local recruiting station. There he may find representatives of all services, if the community is large enough. If he does not have such an installation in his own city, it may be that a larger community less than a hundred miles away does. The miles involved may not be considered too much of a hindrance. Perhaps the pastor fears that the recruiter may only obscure the facts? In most cases such would not be true. The recruiter wants to provide the best possible individual for the military. Such a person has to be well motivated. If his motivation is less than the best, the contribution he will make to the service will certainly be limited. The recruiter is doubly important for he has at hand the regulations that presently apply. He can present accurately the possibilities that are available to the young person who wishes to enlist. He knows the present needs in various categories of experience and training. He knows the military schools that are seeking students. He knows the aptitudes that are most desired. He is a resource person who must not be ignored.

Granted, the recruiter wants men and women for the service. Granted, he wants to do a good job and his efficiency as a recruiter is obviously tied in with the number of people he gets. Granted, the probability that all of these strands of motivation blend together to provide rose-colored glasses for viewing the problem. Yet remember that the program envisioned is one which provides for the participation of many. There will be many sounding boards in the search for the facts, and not just one. There will be a free flow of questions and answers. There will be many opportunities to compare notes. Any tendency of the recruiter to cover over the dark side of service life will be countered by those whose reactions are colored by the negative. There will be those whose errors, if any, will be on the bitter side. Their distortions will help counteract any tendency toward distortions in the other direction. The discerning pastor will set up his program in such a way as to invite the open expression of many varying views.

Another resource is that of the young people in the congregation who have had short periods of service. They should be sprinkled throughout the program as well. Obviously, they will not judge the life of the serviceman as would the man who spent "the best years of his life" in the service, and then retired. They will not see service life as would the recruiter, or the man or woman on active duty who has found the life satisfying on the whole. Their viewpoint must be included in the discussion groups that are set up. The statement of a man who has just completed his involuntary period of enlistment should be sought. All of these views tend to assist the young person in his thinking.

Out of such diverse groups effective panels can be assembled—panels where opposing views cannot be obscured. A panel discussion led by a retired officer, an active-duty enlisted man, a military chaplain, and a recent returnee from a short period of service would make a lively session. The young people can be trusted to evaluate rather carefully. Most young people recognize bad temper when they see it. They also spot quickly any attempts to gloss over facts. They can separate the "Pollyanna" from the embittered. If they are not able to weigh such evidence carefully, all the more reason that they should be given an opportunity. How else can they learn? Certainly the facts they are furnished can only assist them in the long run to make a decision or to face a fact that is forced upon them by life itself. Such a training program will in itself be a time of growth.

Such a program tends to offer its own outline, as the resource people are assembled. Certainly it should contain periods of factual instruction, presented as illustrated lectures with a question period. The facts presented might cover opportunities offered by the various branches of service, schooling possibilities, the demands of overseas assignments, advancement chances, the demands of a typical basic training program, the fringe benefits available to service people, hardship tours and their problems, the structure of military life (comparing enlisted and commissioned opportunities), facts about the military environment (how they might have to live), and many other subjects which would arise in the preliminary planning for the course. The program would also provide many opportunities for discussion, and opportunities for the group to deal with the feelings of its members. Perhaps a session could be arranged at which military doctors, psychiatrists, or psychologists and their civilian counterparts would discuss physical and emotional demands that are inherent in the life of the military. Parents, of course, could be involved in the group work and be present during the periods of factual instruction.

Certainly the program would involve field trips to military installations. Often, not too remote from the local church, there are Army posts, Air Force bases, and Navy or Marine installations. Such visits would give a first-hand opportunity to observe living conditions and the demands of various assignments. The visits must not be allowed to degenerate into mere opportunities to see military equipment, weapons, aircraft, and/or naval vessels on dress parade. They must be oriented toward the purpose of the instruction: a better, more realistic understanding of what is involved in the military service. Since commanders have so much of their time tied up with disciplinary problems among the poorly motivated members of their command, they are usually more than co-operative about attempting to present a realistic picture. They would rather have some men persuaded against a military career. If they could screen out the inadequately motivated, they would be only too glad.

Other Possible Elements of the Instruction

Thus far we have considered only an attempt to get the facts about military life and to assimilate some of them in periods set aside for group work. The facts have been limited to the advantages and disadvantages, demands and opportunities, of military life itself. There are other subjects with which such a training program could deal. Again, the local church is full of resource people and instructional possibilities.

One important area of instruction would involve our national heritage. Chaplains in the military services find that despite courses in history and civics and related subjects, many of our people are totally unacquainted with the nature of our national heritage. Perhaps the schools have been understandably a bit backward about emphasizing the religious roots of many of our democratic ideas. However, the local church need not hold back. Often the instructor in the local school, who has not dealt directly with such matters in the classroom, will feel like expressing his knowledge more emphatically in a voluntary group studying within the environment of the local church.

Such courses can draw upon a wealth of literature dealing with the foundations of our nation. They should, I feel, be fair, and thus should neither glorify nor debunk the very fine traditions that are ours. The course should help people to understand those elements of our national development that are worth defending. It should point up the moral nature of man and the need for a way of life that promotes the activity of the individual conscience. It should point up the need for fair play, good sportsmanship, and basic decency that makes the way of freedom so important. It should not gloss over our mistakes but should emphasize that freedom always leaves room for the correction of mistakes, whereas the totalitarian state perpetuates its errors.

The course would inevitably involve training in the teachings of the Communist world. Such training should not be conducted by members of the extreme right, nor by those with known leftist tendencies. It should be presented in an intellectually respectable way, as objectively as possible. The errors that we feel are a part of the totalitarian state must be pointed out, but also the half-truths that make such an approach seem attractive to the "have-nots" should be made clear. The American prisoners of war who succumbed to Communist indoctrination were weakened by their lack of knowledge as well as by their lack of wholehearted devotion to the American way. We must present the facts, but we must also provide a sense of devotion to the good that underlies our way of life. We must not identify the Western world with a materialism that is better than the totalitarian way only because it is more successful in providing luxuries. Moving away from exalting selfish motivation, we must promote a sense of oneness with a nation whose history is marked by self-sacrifice more than it is marred by the selfish drive toward success in the "thing" world. A series of presentations organized around the present "Code of Conduct" would probably help meet the need that I have been outlining. Films that might assist in such a project are available—possibly through nearby military installations. Some, of course, would have nominal commercial restrictions, but the local church budget can rise to the occasion in most instances.

Such a course could contain some instructional periods dealing with the current posture of the free world against the Communist world. It would provide for the presentation of facts about the current situation in many corners of the world. The need for military strength to provide opportunity for the forces of freedom to develop their own ability to stand alone would become obvious. Such presentations might compel the church involved to rethink the attitude it has toward the military. Certainly such presentations would tend to provide the young person with a sense of purpose that would stand him in good stead during his military service.

If desired, the course might also provide a review of the role of the military in the history of our nation. Such topics as the growth of the citizen soldier concept, the lack of political power on the part of the military in America, and present-day needs for a standing army are worthy of consideration. Such an approach might bring out the contributions that have been made possible through the military, and its part in natural emergencies, floods, earthquakes, fires, and famines —at home and abroad. I am not suggesting that the course be used as an opportunity for recruitment, but I am pointing out that it is possible to stick to the facts and provide a young person with enough motivation to enable him to put his period of military service to good use and to return with a sense of having contributed somewhat to the betterment of the world in which he lives.

Conclusion

The pastor with a true "shepherd's heart" will probably want to provide an opportunity for his young people to meet their military obligations with good grace. He will realize that a knowledge of the facts will help prepare them for serving the nation in a manner that reflects credit upon the church. He will see that as individuals they can be saved by an advance warning from some of the pitfalls that exist in the military service. He will accept the responsibility of the church to meet the needs of the people by providing such a course of instruction. His own implication in the preparation of the course, in the contacts necessary with military and civilian leaders in the community, and in the presentation of the various classes should assist him to grow. After a program of instruction of this nature, he should have a deeper understanding of the role of the Church in the nation and of the commitments which his country has made in the cause of freedom under God. He should have a new sense of identification with the lives of the families of his parish, and he should have a sense of accomplishment that would provide ample reward for his work.

By providing not only for factual presentations, but also for the expression of feelings in small group sessions or private conferences with the young people, the pastor would have helped the participants to grow, whatever their later relationship to the military. He would have made sure that the period of service, compulsory or voluntary, would be a time of maturing which would restore his people to the community even better equipped for the tasks at hand.

CHAPTER NINE

"YOUR CHURCH MISSES YOU"

(The Home Church Follows Her Own)

He read the letter aloud to me: "As I gaze into the setting sun each evening, my thoughts are always of you, and I wish that I could be there and you could be here. . . ." The letter went on, but we stopped for a moment as both of us laughed uproariously. We were in the Philippine Islands during World War II. The letter came from his home pastor in the United States. The good man had simply gone too far. Together, in my friend's tent, we composed a reply beginning: "As I gaze away from the setting sun each evening, my thoughts are of you, and I wish that you could be here, and I could be there. . . ." I don't know if he ever mailed the reply. I hope he did.

That was about nineteen years ago, and I still remember it very clearly. It is an example of what not to do when you have a man from your congregation in the military service, particularly if he is in an area where shots are still being fired in anger. He can spot false sentimentality quickly. But it is important that the local church follow its members through the mails—not as a patronizing gesture replete with purple passages, but as an honest expression of continuing concern.

The concern must be real. I heard of another case during World War II when a man received a pseudopersonal, mimeographed letter from his pastor. The serviceman's reaction was to contact a friend who worked as a clerk and have him cut a stencil for a reply, so that the response was also mimeographed as a form letter. Surely that pastor got the point. It is not enough to set up an administrative procedure that will see that form letters are sent on the way to those members who are in the service. The concern must be genuine and it must be personal.

Of course the local church should send mimeographed or printed materials to those far away, just as it does to those at home. A service-man overseas appreciates a copy of the church paper each time it comes out. It keeps him posted on things going on at home. He also likes to know when the church is making a special plea to all members; in such an instance he understands, just as anyone else would, that a matter of this sort must be handled in the least expensive, most practical way. But the point is that the member away from home in the military service really needs more than that. He needs a personal word from his pastor, the associate pastor, or someone representing the membership of his local church. It is this word that must be personal and genuine. Modern techniques of mass communication must not be utilized to meet these requirements. If they are to be met, they must be met by a person who cares. If your church is "too large" to perform this task, perhaps it is, indeed, too large. Actually, the size is not the controlling factor, for a little bit of careful organization can provide just this personal contact even in our largest of churches. Some of them do a better job than those so small that the pastor, with a little bit of trouble, could do the job himself. The controlling factor is actually "Does the church really care?" and not how large it is.

Importance of Contact with the Local Church

You may say that it is enough that your denomination furnishes chaplains to the military service. Why doesn't a contact with the chaplain meet the need? The answer is that nothing can take the place of the knowledge that "Your home church misses you." A word from home is a word from home (apologies to Gertrude Stein). Now if the chaplain has just visited in your hometown and brings a personal word from a mutual friend, that is a different thing! For here would be a word from home, whereas the mere visit of a unit chaplain in itself would not be the same thing. But the opportunities to bring a personal report of a visit with a mutual friend from the home church are only too rare. The most expeditious way of supplying a truly personal contact from the home church is through a letter, however brief, but nonetheless a genuine expression of personal concern.

Why is it so important that the home church supply these reminders of the personal concern of the church for all its people? Because, I think, there is, in one sense, *no* church but the *local* church.

This does not mean that a person must always have his membership in the church where he first joined. Not at all. Indeed, he should move his membership when he actually changes his residence, and then give his loyalty to that expression of the Church Universal in his new home. I certainly believe that the recent interest of many of the churches in keeping their membership rolls up-to-date is important. The "sentimental" member who has never been home since he left for the big city or who goes back only once a year ought to be encouraged to recognize the error of his ways. It is important for *him* to place his membership where he actually lives, just as it is important for the church. Yet this approach does not apply to the man in the military service. It certainly does not apply to the short-timer in the service whose only desire is to return to his home and stay there. But it also does not apply to the service family, for although they may not come home to live for many years, if at all, they need a church home and the military chapel cannot provide such a home. There is no "Army Protestant Church." The military chaplain ought never to feel a glow of pride when his parishioners tell him "We really don't have a denominational affiliation. We are 'military' and we've always worshipped in military chapels. I guess we belong to the military." It is human to appreciate loyalty, but there are many human feelings which it is dangerous to indulge. The military chapel is simply not a "church." It provides a place of worship for those who belong to the body of Christ, as it also provides a center for instruction and for fellowship. But it is not a "church." It has no membership roll, and it cannot have one. The chapel exists as a joint effort of the United States Department of Defense and the free churches of America to implement the "free exercise" clause of the first amendment to the Constitution of our "great republic." It exists as an expression of the fact that the Church follows her own and as a practical way to provide the services of religion to those in the military service, but it is not a church. This fact is clear to the denominational groups who endorse their clergymen to the military as "chaplains."

Even to those of his congregation who belong to the same denomination as the chaplain, the chapel cannot be a "church." So, if the Church is to follow its members with a continuing expression of personal concern, it must be through the efforts of the home church, mainly through the mails. Such an expression of interest will make the work of the military chaplain much more effective. His contacts in counseling or in conveying messages from home will be immediately more valuable if the person he is visiting has a feeling that his church has not forgotten him for a minute. The chaplain then becomes a bridge to the Church, not just a reminder of those the serviceman once thought cared for him but who apparently have forgotten.

The basic responsibility lies, as always, with the people concerned. How is the pastor to build the bridge to the military chaplain without some building materials? In this instance the materials required are simply information as to what is happening. If the serviceman, or his family, fails to let the pastor know of his entrance into the service, it may take some time before information filters through from other sources. The pastor, however, can help by letting his people know of his continuing interest and his need to be informed. Through information given to new members, through items in the bulletin each Sunday, through the church newspaper, and through personal conversations, the pastor can remind his people of his need to know. The pastor should point out that it is not only the original entrance into the service that he wants to know about but also any significant changes, such as changes of station, when he is promoted, when he is in trouble, and when there are any interesting events in the family, such as the birth of a child. That is, the pastor wishes to know of anything he would be concerned about if the serviceman was at home in the parish.

In addition to his information-seeking efforts, the pastor should review his interest with the serviceman who is reporting for induction, just to make certain that the church is not forgotten in the excitement. Once the very real interest of the home pastor has been emphasized, it is easy for the military chaplain to build on that foundation. When something important, good or bad, happens to the serviceman from such a church background, instead of thinking "Nobody cares," he will immediately think, "My home pastor cares." Perhaps from this point he will go on to think also, "The chaplain cares, I'll tell him."

When the church is "the Church" it is a redemptive community. The Church is the body of Christ still living in this world and ruled by his Spirit. The Church is a bridge from birth to death and beyond death to life everlasting. The Church is a bridge from home to school, or to the hospital, or to the business world. The Church is certainly a bridge from a peaceful life at home where even the headlines of the morning newspaper seem rather unreal, to a life within a military organization directly and immediately responsive to every varying wind from the Communist world. The Church, where she is the Church, has a concern for her people, not as statistics, but as persons. Where she is true to her nature, the Church can never forget these facts. Now, since the Church is most clearly "the Church" in the form of the local church, it is most important that the local church remains true to its nature. When the local church fails, the whole Church fails.

When a local church forgets to care, the power of Christ to care is dimmed in the mind of the one who is forgotten. It becomes that much harder for him to believe that it is all true. The work of the military chaplain becomes difficult. While the local church is so important to the universal Church, it must never think of itself as so important that nothing away from its geographical limits counts. The church, no more than the individual Christian, cannot live for itself alone. The very nature of the church is to reach outward to proclaim its message of love to those whose lives must be lived in difficult circumstances away from the comforts of home. Such "comforts" include not only "luxuries" but those personal relationships that tend to strengthen and encourage and add a deeper sense of meaning to life. This means that the members of the church who are in the military service must not be given cause to think that they are forgotten by those whose nature is to care.

The military is often relegated to the fringes of society. It exists as an arm of society and has no reason for existence except as demanded by the culture it serves. In a democratic nation, the military must never be important for itself alone. It is important in that it provides a cloak of strength behind which our society can develop peacefully. Yet the military is always faced with the fact that peace is not very peaceful in our present world. The military is constantly reminded of the destructive potential in our present world where strife is the rule. And remember that "the military" is people. It is your son, your brother, your husband, your sister, your daughter, your mother, or your father. These people live on the fringes of what may appear to be a peaceful world. Some of them die as they represent those at home whose lives go on on a "business as usual" basis.

Even as this is written there are wives and children whose husbands and fathers are part of what has been called a "dirty, little war." These people must never be led to think that the church at home has forgotten them. The church at home must never play ostrich to the world in turmoil.

How the Local Church Corresponds

What then must be done if the local church is to demonstrate its nature as a community that cares? How is the redemptive love of Christ to be made clearly evident by the home church? If we are to carry on our membership rolls many people who may never be personally available to assist in our program and if our ministry to them is to continue, how is this to be accomplished effectively? I think one clue to a possible solution of the problem is to remember that it is the local church that must remain the Church for those in the service. Then any outreach toward them will stem from that fact. Immediately it is clear that members who are in the military service ought to be included in most of the mailings of the church. They should not be ignored when a new financial campaign is begun. Whatever they are contributing to the work of the military chapel or to charitable enterprises away from home, they still ought to be given an opportunity to identify with the work of the church at home. They must be kept apprised of the fact that since our money is an extension of ourselves as persons we ought naturally to give to the work of the church to which we belong. If we are personally identified with the church to which we belong, we are extended a privilege when we are asked to contribute to worth-while ventures of that church. It must not be felt that to ask those in the service for contributions to the work of *their* church is likely to be misunderstood. For those who really care for the church, a failure to include them in a request is likely to be understood as a rejection by the home church.

In addition to such requests, certainly those in the service ought to receive any publications that provide information about activities and people at home. Of course they won't be able to participate, but it is like a letter from home to see what well-known groups are doing. It is a rare person who will be embittered by the fact that people at home carry on as always. And if he is so self-centered, it is possible that he does not understand the nature of the Church anyway. His feelings must not be favored, else the desires of the vast majority be forgotten. If he is continually well posted as to activities at home, he may someday begin to recognize that such a constant expression of interest means that the church at home really does care.

Now we come to the clearly personal expression of concern, the personal letter. This is the letter that must not be a form letter. It must never be stenciled or printed. It is what it purports to be or it is not effective. If it is anything less than the expression of the concern of a representative individual, it had better not be sent. What is a "representative" individual? First, he is an "individual," a "person." It is the fact that it is a word from "him" that makes the letter "personal." Second, the writer is a man or woman employed by the church (whether paid or unpaid is really not important to the receiver of the letter) to make sure that personal contact is maintained with those far from home. Or it may be that he or she represents one of the groups within the local church (perhaps the president of a Sunday school class or one of the men's or women's groups) and is carrying out the instructions of the group itself. At any rate, the letter must have been written by a person who had the addressee in mind and who was writing to keep him apprised of the fact that "your church misses you." He is a *person* who *represents* other persons in the local church when he writes the letter to the serviceman or his family.

Then comes the question of when to write and for what purposes? To begin with, there is a need for a letter from the home church when the person first goes into the service. He should receive a letter soon after he vanishes into the military. Such a letter should reach him as soon as he has a fairly stable address. A letter from the home church is quite important while he is in basic training or boot camp. A letter from anybody at home is important then, for that matter! This letter should establish the fact that the home church is not going to forget him! The service address can be determined by a call, either in person or by telephone, on the family at home. Such a contact would also reassure the family and make certain that they understand that the church is going to continue to care. Thus the contacts with the service member also strengthen the tie of the family with the church. This initial letter should do something more. It should remind the person of the importance of worshipping either at his chapel or at another church of his denomination in a nearby community. It should also encourage him to go to see his chaplain and to introduce himself.

The effect of this initial letter would be greatly enhanced by a companion letter to the post or base chaplain at the installation to which the military person is assigned. The chaplain there will make sure that the letter is placed in the hands of the unit or area chaplain who is involved. If he answers, as he should, there will be a direct contact set up between the home church and the military chaplain. This should be a great source of help for the serviceman and his family. Such a contact makes it much easier for the military chaplain to be of value at a time of crisis, should one develop. His counseling and other attempts to help will be advanced by the erection of such a bridge between home and the service. The bridge might be even sturdier if it is possible for the home pastor to write the chaplain, particularly if there are known problems that will require assistance. Information might also be included as to any specific interests or talents the serviceman might have. If the chaplain can put those talents to work, or allow the expression and development of those interests, the service person might be strengthened in his personal life.

The initial letter will certainly not do the whole job. But it is a start. To forget to write it is to have to start from behind later. The local church should write the first letter, but it must not consider the job finished until some later crisis arises. Rather, a separate file should be kept so that the service person or family will not be forgotten. Each change of station should be noted and the contact maintained no matter what the number of transfers. Also, if the serviceman is accompanied by his dependents, it should be noted when they are forced to be separated, so that letters may go to both the serviceman and his waiting family. Letters at such times are most important. As has been pointed out in earlier chapters, the enforced separations of military life are critical times for all concerned.

To make sure that letters are sufficient in numbers to maintain contact, the local church should not wait for reassignments or periods of separation. It might well insure that letters, however brief, are sent to mark birthdays, wedding anniversaries (where those are known to the church), and other anniversaries such as those of baptism or confirmation. Also, whenever a home call is made on parents or wives and children still living in the local community, a letter reporting the visit and containing a personal word from the home folks would be valuable. A copy of such a letter could be sent to the family at home. Such a combination of contacts and personal services would only strengthen the ties of the family, the serviceman, and the church to one another.

I believe that such a plan is feasible if the concern is great enough. The representative person can be either a paid member of the staff or a volunteer, performing the service for the church either at home or at the church office. The women of the church are often seeking volunteer work they can perform on their own time. Often a skilled stenographer who has given up the office for the demands of motherhood is only too happy to find a way to put her carefully acquired skills to work for the church. If a separate file is established for servicemen and their families it would be simple to provide the necessary information for those who are to write the letters. If the letter is to be written by someone else but signed by the pastor, he should give enough guidance so that the letter, as it is finally composed, does actually represent his personal thinking on the matter. Such guidance could be given in hastily handwritten notes or dictated into a machine. The actual composition of the letter could then be left to the paid or volunteer worker. A quick reading of the letter before the pastor signs it would assure that it does represent his personal concern. However, I do not believe that it is at all necessary that the pastor himself write and sign the letter. The "representative person" I referred to can carry the total burden. Obviously it would be necessary to interview the person selected to make sure of his qualifications for such a task, but such interviews are accepted as necessary and, indeed, might have the effect of another personal contact with a church member. Certainly such contacts are needed, lest the church become a smoothly operating business machine rather than a living organism in a world so much in need of meaningful personal contacts.

The Local Church and the Chaplain

Another channel of communication that will not require quite so much activity is that of the local church with the military chaplain. However, in this case, a relatively few letters can have an effect far beyond the time and trouble required in writing them. In such letters, where it is known, the chaplain at the larger installation should be furnished the specific unit assignment of the person concerned. The post or base chaplain, who may have thousands within his charge, can immediately place the letter in the hands of the unit or area chaplain concerned. If the local church does not have such information, the chaplain can find it by using his military locater system. The letter might well indicate any special problems or abilities, talents or interests, as mentioned above. Not only are such letters helpful to the chaplain in keeping his program going by providing people for choirs, to serve as ushers for Sunday services, and for the other necessary requirements of an active chapel program, but they are helpful in case it becomes necessary for him to deliver word of emergencies or to provide counseling for any purpose.

The letter really says something more to the chaplain. It tells him that the local church really cares and that if he needs to get word to the family at home, he can write the local pastor and expect a courteous and prompt reply. He can know that if he requests a home visit, the local pastor will either provide it or let him know why it was not considered possible or helpful. As the contact between the home church and the chaplain is developed, it can provide a resource for counseling on a professional level, as pointed out in the chapter on the use of correspondence in counseling.

As the serviceman and/or his family moves about in the period of military service, it is wise for the home church to write a new letter to the chaplain of the next installation concerned. This letter might cover the same ground as the first one, but there might even be more useful information to add. If, at the same time, the chaplain is doing his part and is passing on word that he has about the persons concerned to the chaplain at the next post, a double line of communication has been established so that the concern of the church is certain to be made clear. Letters written when no crisis exists make letters written at a time of crisis much more valuable. As any pastor knows, a personal contact before an urgent need arises, almost always makes the contact in time of trouble more helpful.

Contact beyond Correspondence

The concern of the local church with its own is not limited only to correspondence, whether it be with the chaplain or with the individual away from home. Military people do come home on occasion. In most cases they will make the first gesture by appearing at services of worship or in the church school. If a follow-up is possible, it should be made by a personal contact from some member of the church staff. If the duration of the stay is long enough, a personal interview with the pastor, however brief, would be most significant. When I was first drafted into the Army as the lowest of privates in 1941, I had an opportunity to visit with my pastor, a very busy man with a church of many members. He gave me no advice, he produced no pat answers to my many questions about war and why God allows it, but he certainly made it possible for me to believe that the church cares for her own. The fact that he put aside time in his schedule for me, and the way in which he heard me out, said more to me than thousands of carefully worded theological statements about the nature of the Church could ever say.

Even if the serviceman's assignment precludes a visit to his home town, it is sometimes necessary for his wife and children to return. In such cases, a personal call on them is imperative. The wife will be facing the crisis that separation causes. She will be wondering how she is to care for her family without the man of the house. She will be faced with fears about her husband's welfare. She will need to know that she really is home, and that the circle of concern has closed about her. A written report of that visit, written on a positive note if at all possible, is most important to the man far from home. He needs to know that his loved ones are being cared for by the church. Such knowledge will make it possible for him to keep his relationship to the church at a significant level, and for him to face the dullness of routine, or the dangers of actual combat, with more assurance.

The church at home should keep such contact with its members away from home that it knows when they are returning to stay. A family or an individual returning from military service to civilian life needs immediate assurance of acceptance by groups once well known to them. It doesn't take much, but anything that can be done to assure them that they are, indeed, at home is quite important to them and to the church concerned.

Summary

By now, I am sure that some readers are beginning to rebel. Such a fabric of communication is far too complex to maintain. What church can possibly provide such complete coverage for its people in the military? What work would get done at home? What pastoral calling could be provided for those still active in the program if we bogged down in such an enterprise? Better leave it to the chaplain, that is what he is paid for!

I think I have pointed out clearly that such a program also strengthens the church at home and provides opportunities for pastoral contacts of a significant nature. Such a demonstration of continuing concern for the welfare of those who might otherwise vanish into the military machine is natural to that church which is true to her Master. It is not a question of "whether," it is a question of "how?" I have tried to provide guidelines as to the "how." It is up to the local church to decide how many of the guidelines are applicable. It is up to the local church to devise new guidelines that might be more helpful. It is *not* up to the local church to decide it is unimportant that contact be kept. I think this is clearest when it is remembered that the military chapel is not a "church," although it may represent *the Church*. Only the local church in which the serviceman and his family hold their membership can be *the Church* for them:

CHAPTER TEN

"BUT, PASTOR, HE'S So RESTLESS"
(Readjustment to Civilian Life)

She was an attractive young woman, her beauty somewhat veiled by her expression of bewildered concern. Her voice was rather soft, made so by her struggle to hold back intense emotion while trying to discuss her problems. She had paused for only a few moments, although it seemed to the pastor that the silence was interminable. She went on: "But, pastor, he's so restless. He's just not the same, not the man I married. And it's not only me. Even little Billy, our son, feels it. I know he does! What in the world am I going to do?"

Actually she had already begun one of the first steps. She had sought the advice of her pastor. The moment she began to discuss the problem, she had begun to work on it. It would not be the worst response in the world for the pastor, as he did in this case, to say "Whatever you are going to do will take some time, and you've already started doing what you can—you came to me to talk about your feelings. This will certainly help."

The pastor knew that the hard work on the problem had already begun before Mrs. Ames came to see him. Probably long hours of emotional struggle had already taken place as she strove to keep the problem within the family circle—even within her own heart. She had gotten somewhere, too. She had reached the point where she knew she had to get the problem into the open, and she had come to one trained to keep his mouth shut about other's problems. Instead of making the mistake many make—of talking to well-intentioned "friends" next door or across the street—she had kept her own counsel until she was in the pastor's office. Now it was up to him to provide understanding, emotional support, and a listening ear. As the work progressed, opportunities would come to assist her in her growth toward a more mature relationship with life itself. Anyway, the work had begun.

The Nature of the Problem

The matter was a complex but natural one. Let's take a look at some of the things that had been happening with this couple. First, the marriage itself, which took place when the man was facing military service. Indeed, it was fairly certain that he would not only soon be in the service but would probably be sent overseas before very long. Convinced of the reality of their love and romantically undisposed to wait until the period of service ended, they had married. True, both sets of parents had tried to slow them down but, as usual, such attempts had only served to convince the young couple of the rightness of their decision.

Then came the wedding and several weeks of rather dazed excitement, with only the slightest intimations that problems in adjustment to one another would become increasingly evident as an inherent part of a marriage between two normal young people. Shortly after he went into the service it became evident that a child was on the way. His orders came for an overseas assignment. He explored alternate possibilities with his commander and his chaplain, and there was nothing to do but go. Away from home and faced with the demands of a military environment, the young man naturally continued to work, beneath his own awareness, on the basic problem of his generation. He was still young enough to be involved predominantly in the asking of the question, "Who am I?" As he worked toward such an acceptance of himself that he could move beyond that basic question to the matter of giving himself to others without fear of losing his own identity, he certainly did change. Change on a background of continuity is the law of life. Dave Ames remained the same person, but not in the same way. He had to adjust to a system of group life structured by clear-cut authority relationships. He had to adjust to life in a peculiarly male atmosphere. He learned the "hypocrisy of roughness," the product of a tacit conspiracy to deny sensitivity of feelings. Men shout at one another. The curses, hurled back and forth in the barracks or in the BOQ, if taken at their face value, would insure a fight to the death. However, they are ordinarily accepted for what they are, only a way of showing friendliness without admitting it.

Under such circumstances, qualities recognized by our culture as "male" are stressed. The ranks are closed, and women tend to become the enemy against whom all campaigns are directed. Women, like ships, are to be sighted and sunk. The existence of strong feelings of mature love toward a wife are kept out of sight, only to be discussed with an extremely select few. When men live solely with men, modesty gets lost. Such things as love of beauty and a subtle reaction to the expression of feeling in great literature also get lost in the man-swarm. Independence, aggressiveness, cynicism, and the suppression of most emotions (with the exception of anger) are part of the military environment.

It is true, of course, that other aspects of personality are still present and do find, in most cases, a way to express themselves. The serviceman works in a craftshop and with loving care shapes a cabinet for a record player, or polishes stones to bring out their beauty and to make from them a bit of jewelry for his wife or his mother. He listens to good music, if he has any inclination in that way, and his response to beautiful sound is even deepened. A good film or a good book will tend to awaken an honest response in most men and thus assist them to develop more fully. But all of these aspects of experience are played down while in the service. And the interesting fact is that the personal attributes that are restrained in a strictly male world, are the very qualities of character that would contribute stability to a well-founded marriage. It is not strange that Mrs. Ames, for example, found her husband to be a "different" man. The fact that he was also the *same* man is a fact that would come out in the counseling over a period of time.

Dave had, by his actions, asked his environment, "Who am I?" and he got back an answer. Like all humans, desiring to be accepted by the group, he had shaped his questions to get a feedback of worth from those around him. He got the answer, "You are a good buddy, a man to tie to, and a *real man*." The answer he got stimulated him to continue to develop in that direction. Thus his sense of worth grew and was reinforced by the group.

Then the longed-for day came. He got out of the service and went home to be with his wife and with the baby he really did not know. He understood the fact that he did not know his own child. What he did not understand was the fact that he did not really know the wife to whom he returned. This became evident within the first week or two. Those first moments of reunion were so physically electric that all else was obscured. It was good to be home. Then came the frustration of recognizing how difficult it was to talk to one another. Outbursts of temper followed when the child would not or could not sleep. Then came the bewilderment of being turned down by his wife when he wanted to make love. How difficult it was for him to know that mothers get tired beyond the limits of desire, that in some measure the sexual drive of the mother is met by her physical handling of the baby. Above all, he had forgotten that he was changing—and so was his wife.

In a very natural way, Betty had been asking the same questions Dave asked: "Who am I?" "Am I worth something?" "Can I trust myself enough to give myself to another?" and other similar queries. But her answers had been coming from quite a different environment. The baby said to her in many demanding ways, as well as in many delightful ways, "You are a mother." Sometimes that answer wasn't well received. It is difficult for a young woman who has been pampered by her parents and whose ego has been inflated by her husband in the courting period of their life to bow to the fact that living is most demanding. This fair daughter of the graces, whose presence was a whiff of fragrant perfume, now has her head in the water closet much of the day as she rinses out diapers. This child, whose health was the constant concern of her parents, now has to keep going no matter what. However tired she is, she must get up to change the baby or to feed him. However dull the routine of every day, she must take care of the infant's needs. Our urban, apartment-style culture offers little support. No longer can a mother get a change in pace by simply leaving the little one to aunts or uncles or cousins or nieces on the farm. She must find her own baby-sitter and she must find the money to pay for the service. Even if "mama" lives only across town, it is still across town, and "mama" is not always overjoyed by the prospect of cancelling her bridge club to act as sitter for the grandchild.

Betty Ames has been asking life to tell her who she is and the answer has led her in another direction from her husband's. She has had to be more than "mother." She has had to be "father" as well. Decisions Dave would have made had he been at home, she must make. She has to make financial decisions, even decisions as to where she will live if it becomes necessary to move while Dave is gone. She must decide what to do about the car that was so wonderful while they were in school, but which is getting to be a financial drag without Dave around to tinker with it and keep it going. She decides what groups of people will constitute her social set. A sympathetic young woman whom she'd not known before the baby came, becomes her best friend. She spends what time she can get away from the baby with her new friends and the new faces that go with them. Betty must strive to carry on without a husband to lean upon except through the mails, which is not quite the same thing. She can't, or at least she *should* not, put her head on the mailman's shoulder and cry it out.

What happens is that Betty learns to get along without a man. Her development takes her toward independence, toward a recognition that she has the strength to carry on. She gets used to ordering her life around her baby and herself, and it is not easy for her to get used to Dave when he returns. After the ardor of the first moments cools, the irritation caused by new demands becomes evident. Betty was not aware of it, but when she told of her husband's changing, she also said, "I have changed." It is not strange that such couples have difficulties in getting together after a long separation. It is only strange that so many do as well as they do. The pastor must plan to provide time and energy to enable Betty and Dave to work toward a more responsible, yet more rewarding, relationship.

Somewhat the same beginning to a counseling session can develop with quite a different situation. Granted this second case is not as common as the matter of Dave and Betty, yet it happens in increasing numbers in our society. This is the case of an older woman whose husband has spent from twenty to thirty years in the service and is now retired. In a measure the problem here is the same as it is with any retired person. There are, however, some differences due to the regimented life of the military. At present, such cases are becoming fairly commonplace on the American scene, since many men whose service began with World War II are reaching the time for retirement. So many senior military men are getting out now, and will be in the years immediately ahead, that it is creating a problem for the military. If younger leaders cannot somehow be encouraged to remain until retirement, the military services are in for trouble. Civilian pastors in America need to be conscious of the problem so that they may prepare to assist the old "mossback" with the problem of adjustment.

When a man has found the military life so satisfactory that he stays in long years, he ordinarily moves up either toward the top of the commissioned ranks or becomes a top "NCO." In either case he gets used to being obeyed. He also gets used to holding a lot of hostility within, when those above become apparently "unreasonable." His position in his unit is rigidly reinforced. His insignia of rank and his ribbons accumulated through years of service tell him just who he is. He knows where he fits in the chain of command. He adopts an almost mechanical response to those above and below him. He knows when to be subservient and when to be demanding. Sometimes he takes out on those beneath him the feelings he has to hold in check toward those above. He may still find some of these adjustments to necessity difficult, but he has had to develop a toleration for them. The fact that such adjustments are made at a cost becomes evident when you listen to the plans of senior military men for retirement. "I'm going back to the family farm and I ain't ever going to town," one says. Another says, reflectively, "I'm going to get a house where no one knows me and I'm going to have nothing to do with anyone unless I decide to on my own." Years of having to be responsive to the demands of those above and below are evidenced in such statements.

The retired military man in a civilian community is like a bank president on a desert island. He just doesn't fit, and he knows it. Restless? Yes, indeed. And if he does not work out a satisfactory adjustment, he's in for trouble. It is interesting to note how many men who have always wanted to retire are unable to handle the fact of retirement. They become restless, apathetic, and seem to lose a will to live. Somehow they must relate effectively to the new environment and begin to get a feedback of worth from it.

The wife of the retired serviceman, like the wife of the retired anybody, has her own problems. She has learned through the years how to get along fairly independently of her husband. She has had much time to herself while he was overseas, or while he was caught up in the demands of his job. Despite the feeling of some civilians that a "peace-time" army has little to do, the average serviceman with the responsibilities that accrue to him through his years of service is busy day, night, and week ends. If he is not overseas, he is away weeks at a time on maneuvers or field problems. He has to adjust to those over him, and often their demands are more stringent than any of the demands of family. Under such circumstances, the wife has had to learn how to live alone and like it. Her activities have been directed toward the wives' clubs, various chapel groups, and other "welfare" activities. Her energies have been exhausted by the proliferation of activities that takes place within the organizations. And, after all those years, suddenly she has a husband who is actually at home. What in the world to do with him? He is demanding, irritable, moody, and just damned difficult. And, worst of all, he is there all of the time! Again it is amazing that the problems are as few as they are! It is certainly *not* amazing that some couples get into serious difficulties just at the time of life when their mutual companionship should have provided an antidote to loneliness.

In addition to the individual restlessness described above, there is also, for the couple that has gone the full course in the military, a shared restlessness. They have had no roots down for so long that they are permanent "tumbleweeds." Every wind of fancy takes them somewhere else in their memories. Where are they to retire? Their parents are dead. Their relatives have never been very close to them. There are *many* communities they remember with some affection. If they have owned a house it has been one purchased when there were no government quarters available and rentals were scarce and exorbitant. It was only a house, and not a home. Thomas Wolfe was right, "You can't go home again." And you certainly can't if home is an organization and a way of life of which you are no longer a part.

Once a decision is reached and an attempt is made to put down roots, it is found that, like the tumbleweed, the roots have shriveled away and have lost their power to go down deep. Then comes the question, "Why did we settle here—why didn't we go somewhere else?" Sometimes it is asked of one another with some intensity, "Why did *you* decide we ought to stay here?" And then there is trouble. There is much for the pastor to work on in such cases, it is true. That is, if he is ever sought out.

To make such problems even worse, the military man with long years of service has developed a sense of pride in the fact that he has "never had to go to the chaplain." The wife often feels the same way. The rigidity of age and habit makes it difficult for them to seek help, and often they settle down to a form of marital cold war for the rest of their lives together. It is tragic, for such a partial resolution of the problem is unnecessary. A pastor with some understanding and some ability in counseling might spell the difference between smoldering resentment toward life and a sense of satisfaction in the evening of life. It is not true that older people cannot be helped through the counseling process. Such a false maxim simply offers a way out for the young pastor who feels inadequate when he is working with those whose experience in living transcends his own. If he does not accept failure, if he persists, he will find that he has something to offer beyond the measure of his own limited experience. His role as a clergyman, invested as it is with the emotions that cluster around one representing a way of life that is older than history and that reaches on beyond death itself, is able to assist him in his work with others far older, and even far wiser, than he.

What to Do about It

We have reached the point in our considerations where the military chaplain becomes rather unimportant. He is graduating his own men into the world of the civilian community. When it comes time for the chaplain to go into that "larger" world, he will have somewhat the same problems that his people face. It is hoped that religion itself will be an aid in making the adjustment, but the need to adjust can be avoided by no one.

What the chaplain can do to assist in the problem of readjustment to civilian life is to work as hard as he can to prepare his people for the fact that there will be problems. The young man often feels that his problems are all related to the military. If he can only get home and out of the service, then all of life will be roses without thorns. Even if he has been mature enough in the military to realize that his problems there are not to be solved by being tried on another job or transferred to another unit, he may still feel that the final move out of the military will take away all pain.

Even the old "fire horse" falls heir to this bit of fantasy. He likes to think how wonderful it will be to be free of responsibility. If he can only go to sleep at night and know that there will be no telephone call in the middle of the night taking him away on some real or fancied emergency! He likes to dream about being able to tell someone to go to blazes when he is asked to do something. He turns over in his mind, with some pleasure, the glory that could come from being free to select his own friends. He hopes, with the poet, to be able to "buy himself a silkworm and listen to it think." And his wife may encourage him in that direction because she has had to put up with the tyranny of the unadmitted feminine "chain of command." Her responses and her friends have been predetermined by her desire to further her husband's career. She, too, has functioned effectively at some cost to herself. In her mind's eye is the joy of cutting some inadequate female dead without having to worry about her husband's job. The two, working together, can conjure up as many fantasies as a youthful couple, if not more.

The chaplain will rarely have a clear-cut opportunity to deal with this problem. He can, however, look for openings. He has, of course, his sermons in which he can approach the problem. And he should make use of them, from time to time, in urging his people toward maturity. Perhaps he will never preach a sermon specifically on separation or on retirement from the service, but every sermon provides an opportunity to touch on related matters that might be helpful. Through the years, maybe some of it will get through. We know that it does. However, he is not limited to such opportunities. Perhaps few will seek him out for counseling because they are concerned about life outside of the Army in the near future, but he has other pastoral contacts. A pastor is always a pastor with his people. He can use friendly contacts, chance conversations, and pastoral calls to provide his people with opportunities for growth. And he should do so. Of course he must not be heavy-handed about it. Nothing would kill off his effectiveness more than a tendency to "preach" in his personal contacts. But, if his own attitudes are positively molded by his faith and his experience so that they are a part of his basic approach to life, he will be able to get it over to others without their realizing what happened.

If the ability of the chaplain to help has suddenly to come to an end, the need is met by the fact that the responsibility of the local pastor moves to fill up what might become a vacuum. Resources within the local church are helpful. Few cases will become "counseling" cases for the pastor, but many can be assisted in other ways. These ways exist and are put to work in many churches quite naturally. In many cases such assistance is provided without the reflective knowledge of pastor or people that such steps are being taken. The very structure of most churches offers help to any who will take advantage of it. There are the natural groups of church life—the church school classes. For the young person returning from the service there is the "post-college" class or the "young married couples" class. Such groups usually contain people who are working through similar problems. The young persons find that they are not alone. They find others facing the same problems, and they know themselves to be understood. The mere knowledge of being understood is a tremendous boost for most of us. In addition to being understood, they find that such groups in their programs find time for people who are trained to help others with various problems. Job opportunities in the local community become evident, opportunities for adult education are pointed up, and various interest groups in the region are made known. Wholesome recreational activities are provided. Such activities, from square dancing to week-end retreats, provide an opportunity for individuals and couples to find their place in the affections of others. The group itself may have come to life without any planned idea of meeting so many varied needs, but the result naturally occurs when like seeks like.

However, the way in which such groups meet the needs of their people can be seen when it is carefully reflected upon. Once a pastor understands something of the way such groups meet needs, he will make certain that they are formed and that they are supported where necessary by the local church.

For the older person, the problem may be more difficult. So many of the groups of older people are made up of those who have grown up in the same community and have been absent from the local scene for only short periods of time. Such groups tend to be "in-groups." It is often difficult to get their members to open their hearts to new people. Yet it can be done. If the pastor is aware of the problem, and if he has a shepherd's heart, he can get his attitude over to his people. If he is only concerned with his group as it is, and he has known it through the years, the groups within his church will tend to be as cold as he is.

The pastor should talk over such matters with his director of religious education. In most cases the director will also be aware of such problems and only too willing to work on a solution.

One of the major problems of our time is how to provide for the needs of our senior citizens. With the increase in the ability of the medical world to keep the old machine going, there develops a need to be able to give the machine a reason for operating. The problem, according to Russell Dicks, is not how to add years to life, but how to add life to years. Recent studies have shown that some of our former views toward the later years of life need to be revised. Older people can learn. Older people do change. Older people are still individuals. Older people do have the wisdom of experience. Older people are actually needed by a civilization if it is to avoid making the same mistakes over and over. Our worship of youth must be re-oriented. The answer to our problems does not lie in the application of more physical energy on the part of the young and vigorous. Such an undisciplined application of energy could be the end of civilization as we know it. The patience and the discipline of emotionally healthy older persons are necessary for the health of the world. The ability to reflect seriously and to make haste slowly, which is often the property of the aged, is a quality to be valued in our world. Thus the need to provide for the retired person or couple becomes not a fine, charitable gesture toward the needy, but a move dictated by our own desperate need. With such a motivation, it would be a poor pastor who did not encourage his church to rise to the occasion.

In most communities there is an ever enlarging pool of older people whose abilities, talents, and attitudes are important to the welfare of all. A group of senior citizens should be organized for individuals and for couples. It seems to me that such groups need not be open only to the married or only to the single, but to both. The companionship of both sexes is important, and the number of self-contained couples is less. In such groups new lives can be started. But, however the groups are formed, such groups are necessary. While it is true that elder individuals are still individuals, they also have mutual problems with others in the same age group. They can draw strength from a pool of strength, if it is made available. Those only recently retired, for instance, can be helped by others who are farther along in making the transition. Not only is assistance found for practical adjustments, such as where to live or where to work, but support is offered for the emotional problem of facing a new life in later years. Such groups are a natural part of a church school. They should be provided without undue comment and without unnecessary attention being drawn to the reasons for their existence. There must be no breath of patronage nor any sense of reaching down to help the needy. The best way to avoid such an attitude is to square off with the facts. Our need for the older citizen is much greater than his need for us. Anything we can do to help him adjust to our community is helping ourselves. We will gain much more from such efforts than they will. Yet there is mutual gain.

The pastor has other responsibilities than simply to make sure that the structure of his church provides groups for senior citizens, groups that are not limited to Sunday or to strictly church activities. Much has been accomplished where such groups are made available, but there is more to do. In his calls, the pastor must be alert to the needs of older couples and individuals. He must not assume that because their physical needs are met and because they have already led full lives, they have no other needs. He must make sure that they know of the opportunities within the church for close contacts with others facing similar problems. He must work to relate them to such groups in a friendly, helpful way. He must make more than one visit to the older people he finds. He should recognize that even if he never relates them effectively to the groups he thinks good for them, he can perform a useful function by providing them a listening ear while they work on their feelings in his presence. His knowledge, experience, and the fact of his being a minister can be used indirectly to help those who might never be conscious of their need to be helped.

Out of such contacts may grow an easy transition into a group of persons facing some of the same problems. But counseling relationships also can develop from such contacts. The pastor must be alert to such needs. He must not decide that the need has to be met in only one way, such as by relating those concerned to a group. He must be awake to the varying needs of the individuals he serves. Perhaps a counseling relationship may lead to a later involvement in some group within the church. It is difficult to know. All that can be known is that another person has a need to grow, and that the counseling session is one way to help. Provide for that need and let the future rest where it does anyway—with God!

Yet other needs may develop. Even if a retired serviceman, for instance, has enough money to live without working, he may still need a job if he is to feel worth while. His need for a job may mesh with the need of the community for people with his experiences. It is not the pastor's task to be a vocational counselor, but it is his task to know that such trained people exist and that their work can be helpful to older persons, as well as to young men and women in the early stages of seeking a career.

There is a point here that is being recognized by some denominations. As the church needs more pastors who are free to do their pastoral work, so a need exists for people to assist with the administrative tasks of the churches. If the administrative load can be passed on to others, perhaps more qualified than the pastor for such tasks, the work of the church as a redemptive community has been helped. Some churches are now turning to the retired service person to meet that need. The service person retires, on the whole, at an earlier age than others. He has ability and the stamina to carry a full load. Many servicemen and women have come to recognize the importance of the Church in the world, if there is to be a world at all. They are seeking areas of work where they can feel that they have a share in the work of "peace-making" in our world. They have enough money to select areas of work. They are not pushed by the tyranny of financial need. If they are shown areas where their work will be important and purposeful, they are quick to respond. In some denominations, the agency that endorses chaplains to the military is working on the matter of the placement of retired men in church-related jobs. They are not limiting their interest to the chaplains who are returning, for often their problem is simply the reorientation of their ministry within the civilian framework. Such efforts are important, and it is hoped that the movement will spread. Certainly it is important to the returning individuals, but it is equally important to the church.

Conclusion

Obviously the pastor has an important task in assisting young people, married or single, when they are separated from the service. He has an equally important task, although limited to fewer people, with the senior citizen who retires from the military service. His task is simpler with those who have always had a significant relationship with the Church, but, if he is a true shepherd, he will also work effectively with those whose life has not included the Church until this moment. The pastor's work includes the organization of his church school, the planning of his pastoral calling, and his availability for personal counseling. In other words, both the pastor and the church should be alert to the needs of all who need help.

CHAPTER ELEVEN

A FINAL WORD

(Summary and Conclusion)

Nearly ten years ago I decided to leave the military service. I was so sure of my decision that I had already started working toward a specific assignment to a local church in my home area. My bishop was working on the problem. My mother was expecting to have her grandchildren near enough to watch them grow. Then I changed my mind. This hurt my mother but was a relief for the bishop.

Shortly after my sudden reversal of my earlier decision, I attended my annual conference. There I renewed old friendships and developed new ones. There I was also faced by the cold gaze of the "militant" pacifist, who sternly posed the question: "How can you, a man of God, wear the uniform of a group that exists to kill?" This question could be put another way, so as to include the pacifist, for one can well ask, "How can you, a man of God, continue to belong to the human race?" It was also at this meeting that a well-meaning older friend, a man with many years in the service of the church, said, "We had hoped you were going to come back to the ministry!"

In the early years of my ministry, before my military service as a chaplain, an elderly friend, whose perceptive intellect had always awed me, advised me not to get off into any area of specialized work, but to stay related to the whole work of the church. By this he meant that he felt it would be a mistake to accept anything but the role of a civilian pastor in a local church. Yet, with all respect to him and to my well-meaning friends in the conference, it seems to me that a military chaplain neither leaves the ministry nor impairs his relationship to the work of the whole Church.

It is true that he may be apparently forgotten by his old friends at home. It may be true that he has to work at times to remind himself that the Church cares for him, and that he represents Her. "Out of sight, out of mind," does seem to be a more accurate reporting of the facts than, "Absence makes the heart grow fonder." But it is not true that he ever leaves the Church. He performs for the Church a difficult task. He lives to remind people who are caught up in the necessary dirty work of the world that God does not forget any of His own. The chaplain proclaims by his very presence that God does not wait for men to learn to live together in peace before He grants peace of soul. God continues to grant peace in the midst of discord, love in the midst of hate, hope in the midst of despair, and light in the midst of darkness.

Such a witness is not an easy one, and often the chaplain forgets for the moment the very truths that his presence within the military proclaims. Yet, in the main, the importance of his role remains clear to him. If it did not he would, had he any shreds of conscience remaining, be forced to get out. To remain in the military after losing his vision of the need for the presence of one who represents God is spiritual death for the chaplain and for many with whom he serves.

It is easy for the chaplain to come to believe that no one at home cares or even remembers him. In the busy life of the civilian pastor, the emphasis is focused on local problems. Since the chaplain is not there, he may not be thought about very often; even the chaplain's own personal contacts with friends and church officials at home become infrequent. Such being the case, it is easy for the chaplain, particularly if he has the slightest paranoid tendency, to build up a clear charge against his denomination. It seems to me, however, that the chaplain himself seldom does anything on his part to maintain his connections with those at home. He is more willing to complain to visiting denominational representatives about such matters than to write to those he'd like to hear from. Often the chaplain who complains the loudest is the one who does not bother to answer the letters that he does get.

This book is intended to be one way of opening the channels of communication with the church at home. It is intended as a move toward mutual understanding. I have attempted to portray the people I serve where I serve them but have recognized that this is possible only by trying to understand their relationships with those at home. While focusing on the people we, as ministers, serve, it has seemed necessary to me to strive to understand our relationship to one another. It is my hope that the magic will take place that another has described by saying, "Whenever I struggle to understand another, I somehow have the feeling that I am understood."

This book has not delved into theology, nor has it spent much time in speaking overtly about God. Yet it is deeply concerned with both. It seems to me that the Church is a complex organism expressed through the simplest of relationships. The Church deals with man individually, but recognizes that an individual has no existence except in relationship to others. This is simply John Wesley's recognition that the Bible knows nothing about solitary religion. Man exists in relationship. His basic relationship is to God, but that basic relationship can only be expressed in this world by the quality of his relationship to other children of God. We cannot, for instance, hate our brother and maintain the fiction that we love God.

On the other side of the picture we are brought into an effective relationship with God by the quality of some contact we have had with men. The Church is the redemptive community. People are saved into the Church. Salvation is not an event by which God snatches people out of relationship to others. We are saved *for* others, and not *from* others. Thus the emphasis of this book has been on striving to understand how we are related to others, and how any tampering with our relationships tends to disturb us. Thus if one is suffering from a broken relationship in his life, one way to offer healing is to provide another healthy relationship within which healing can take place. The new relationship, that of chaplain and counselee, does not take the place of the old one. It rather provides the strength to mend the old. But not only to mend it. Rather to mend it in such a way that it has a new quality of maturity resistant to future breaks.

Counseling, such as that envisioned in these pages, is not magic. It is not a way of dramatically erasing the mistakes of the past. It is a way of demonstrating the love of God in such a way that individuals find a new worth within themselves. Wounded and in pain, they are provided an atmosphere of love in which to convalesce. Perhaps the process can be understood in reference to the parable of the Prodigal Son. The young man has thrown away his fortune and possibly injured his health. He may well have created certain destructive habits that have not totally lost their power over him. He, undoubtedly, has brought back the added burden of a tortured conscience. He is physically and emotionally in pain. His return to the farm has not miraculously changed all of that. Only one main fact is different. He is now at home. He has returned to the circle of his father's love. He can work out his problems during the difficult days ahead with the constant reassurance that he is at home among those who care. In the military service, the chaplain must strive to provide a similar environment of compassionate concern, so that those with whom he works can know that they are at home with God.

It is clear, I think, that what I have described about the chaplain's work is true also of that of the civilian pastor. There is, in a sense, no specialized ministry. We are all in the same ministry of God's redeeming love. To understand this is to understand one another more deeply. If we can understand both our people and ourselves more deeply, we can certainly mediate God's love more effectively.

While much of the burden of this book has been in the direction of better understanding, an attempt has also been made to provide some practical advice as to how to put that understanding to use within the framework of the local church. An exploration of the pastor's role as a representative person has been accompanied by a study of the use of the various groups within the church. It is my belief that the natural organization of the vital local church already contains the needs of health that most of our people require. Consciously reflecting on how such healing takes place ought to help the pastor, whether military or civilian, to exploit more fully the resources he already has.

Granted the insights are partial and the practical advice limited, nonetheless some ground has been broken in an area of experience that involves an ever increasing percentage of the people we serve. Military service for the many is the rule in our generation. We must not think of the years in service as a suspension of the laws of growth for a period of time. We cannot turn our back on apparent personality changes that take place in a time of testing. The military, like any other way of life, provides possibilities either for growth or for deterioration. Man goes one way or the other. He cannot stand still. We must learn all we can about how to assist him in the direction of growth. Perhaps this book will stimulate others, more qualified, to help us all toward a better understanding of how we are to serve one another in the name of God.

BIBLIOGRAPHY

ALLPORT, GORDON W., *Pattern and Growth in Personality*. New York: Holt, Rinehart & Winston, Inc., 1961.

BACHMANN, C. CHARLES, *Ministering to the Grief Sufferer*. Englewood Cliffs, N.J.: Prentice-Hall, Inc., 1964.

CRYER, NEWMAN S., JR. and JOHN M. VEHYNINGER, *Casebook in Pastoral Counseling*. Nashville: Abingdon Press, 1962.

CURRAN, CHARLES A., *Counseling in Catholic Life and Education*. New York: The Macmillan Company, 1952.

DICKS, RUSSELL L., *Pastoral Work and Personal Counseling* (rev. ed.). New York: The Macmillan Company, 1949.

————, *Principles and Practices of Pastoral Care*. Englewood Cliffs, N.J.: Prentice-Hall, Inc., 1963.

EISENSTEIN, VICTOR W., ed., *Neurotic Interaction in Marriage*. New York: Basic Books Inc., 1956.

FRANKL, VIKTOR E., *The Doctor and the Soul*. New York: Alfred A. Knopf, Inc., 1957.

GARRETT, ANNETTE, *Interviewing, Its Principles and Methods*. New York: Family Service Association of America, 1942.

GINZBERG, ELI and others, *The Ineffective Soldier*, 3 vols. New York: Columbia University Press, 1959.

HILTNER, SEWARD, *Pastoral Counseling*. Nashville: Abingdon Press, 1949.

————, *Preface to Pastoral Counseling*. Nashville: Abingdon Press, 1958.

HOWE, REUEL L., *The Creative Years*. Greenwich, Conn.: Seabury Press, Inc., 1959.

LOOMIS, EARL A., *The Self in Pilgrimage*. New York: Harper & Row, Publishers, 1960.

MCNEILL, JOHN T., *A History of the Cure of Souls*. New York: Harper & Row, Publishers, 1951.

MENNINGER, KARL, *Theory of Psychoanalytic Technique*. New York: Basic Books Inc., 1958.

MOWRER, O. HOBART, *Crisis in Psychiatry and Religion*. Princeton, N.J.: D. Van Nostrand Co., Inc., 1961.

MUDD, EMILY H. and ARON KRICH, eds., *Man and Wife*. New York: W. W. Norton & Company, Inc., 1957.

MUDD, EMILY H. and others, eds., *Marriage Counseling: A Casebook*. New York: Association Press, 1958.

OATES, WAYNE E., ed., *An Introduction to Pastoral Counseling*. Nashville: Broadman Press, 1959.

————, *Protestant Pastoral Counseling*. Philadelphia: Westminster Press, 1962.

————, *Where to Go for Help*. Philadelphia: Westminster Press, 1957.

ROGERS, CARL R., *Client Centered Therapy*. Boston: Houghton Mifflin Company, 1951.

SHIPP, THOMAS J., *Helping the Alcoholic and His Family*. Englewood Cliffs, N.J.: Prentice-Hall, Inc., 1963.

WHEELIS, ALLEN, *Quest for Identity*. New York: W. W. Norton & Company, Inc., 1958.

WINTER, GIBSON, *Love and Conflict*. New York: Doubleday & Company, Inc., 1958.

YOUNG, RICHARD K., *The Pastor's Hospital Ministry*. Nashville: Broadman Press, 1959.

INDEX

INDEX

Advice giving, 19
Aggression,
  expression of, 22
  resolving feelings of, 23
  toward "father," 24
Al-Anon, 81
Alcohol and the wife, 80 ff
Alcoholics, 20, 71 ff
Alcoholics Anonymous, 78
Alcoholism, 71
Allen, Fred, 27
Aloneness, 22
Anxiety
  "free, floating," 39 ff
  letters, 25, 27
  prevention of, 61
  separation, 39 ff
Authority problems, 16, 18, 20,
  22, 23, 30

Bachmann, C. Charles, 66

Change
  within limits, 24
Chapel & chapel activities, 31, 32
Chaplain
  and correspondence, 51
  as the church, 19, 111
  authority problems, 23
  bridge to the familiar, 46
  delivery of death messages, 60
  identification with authority, 26
  moral influence of, 23
  problems in work with soldier,
    33 ff

Chaplain (cont.)
  role of, 59, 94, 134
  use of "system," 26
Chaplain's assistants
  selection of, 50
Character
  development, 34
  guidance council, 31
  guidance program, 20, 75
Children, 21
Church
  and nation, 107
  education, 100
  follows her own, 108 ff
  past relationship with, 46
  redemptive community, 81, 111,
    135
  represented by chaplain, 19, 20
  sense of purpose, 81
  socials, fellowship gatherings,
    31, 32
Clarification
  a mutual task, 48
  in communication, 38
Commander
  father, 34
  helper, 30
  his resources, 31
  temperance, 76
  the community, 102
Communication(s)
  breakdown of, 21
  long distance, 39 ff
  problem of, 38
  technique of, 52 ff

Conscience
  and self-centeredness, 41
  and sexual loyalty, 42
Correspondence, 21
Counseling
  by letter, 53
  directive, 18
  emergency, 28
  how to use letters, 55, 56
  long term relationship, 28
  marital, 48
  non-directive, 18
  sexual overtones in, 23
  training for, 94, 95
Counselor
  helpful attitude, 57
  identification with authority, 26
  identification with counseling, 23
  pastoral counselor's schedule, 49
  of serviceman and family, 34
  press of schedule, 49
  problems of, 17
  reaction to long distance correspondence, 39

Death messages
  how to deliver, 60 ff
Dependency, 19, 27
Depression
  gloomy letters, 38 ff
Dicks, Russell, 64, 130
Do-gooders
  smugness of, 32
Drinking
  problem or heavy, 71 ff
Dullness, 27, 29

Ericson, Erik, 97

Facing feelings, 56
Finances
  control of, 45
Financial matters, 21
Financial problems, 51, 83 ff
Freudian bit, 41

Gambler, compulsive, 93
Gleason, Jackie, 41
God
  attitude toward, 94
  clergyman and, 17
  difference from man, 42
  forgiving love, 82
  given nature, 43
  hostility toward, 67
  need of clergyman to play, 50
  over identification with, 49
  presence of, 46
  problems with, 16
  source of compassion, 54
Grief
  and separation, 65, 66
  expression of, 62
  glossing over, 65
  need for privacy, 62, 63
  prayer, 63
Group
  concept, 51
  peer, 32
  spirit, 31
Guilt feelings, 16

Helping persons, 17
Hemingway, Ernest, 41
Homosexual, latent, 98

Immorality
  pressure toward, 29
Information
  exchange of, 38
  use of verbatim style to convey, 54

Jesus
  being like, 42

Leader
  morally responsible, 75
  need for, 34
  tendency to downgrade, 34
Linderman, Eric, 66
Loneliness, 21, 22, 23, 46

Man
  as created by God, 42
Marital problems, 21
Maugham, Somerset, 41
Mental hygiene, 31
Morality
  moral welfare, 28
  of fear, 30
  pressures against, 29
  standards, 28
Motivation
  for long term counseling, 28
  for marriage, 43
  for military career, 102
  of helper, 17

NCO
  as helper, 30
  big brother, 34
  importance, 34, 73
  resources, 31

Over-identification
  problem of, 54, 55, 88
Overpsychologizing of problem, 47

Passive individual, 18
Pastor
  alcohol problems, 80 ff
  always a pastor, 128
  and authority problems of clergy-
    men, 23
  and chaplain, 18
  and correspondence, 51
  handling grief in service fami-
    lies, 68 ff
  ministry to serviceman and
    family, 19
  need to understand serviceman's
    situation, 47
  over-identification with God, 49
  preparation for life, 99 ff
  referral to, 41
  schedule, 49
  with retired service couples, 128
Platoon leader, 33, 34

Projection
  in alcohol problems, 77
  in marital separations, 41

Rapport
  establishment of, 34
  need for, 34
Recording tapes
  exchange between counselors, 54
Red Cross
  cooperation with, 25, 27
  delivery of death messages, 60
  in financial matters, 93
Reductionism, 17
Referral, attempted, 37, 38
Rejection
  and wife's independence, 45
  judgmental, 46
Relationship
  and the church, 134 ff
  broken, 38
  helping, 34
  in financial problems, 94
  of acceptance and understand-
    ing, 43
  of mature trust, 46
  with mother, 27
Routine
  coping with, 26
  difficult, 27

Salvation
  by works, 42
  only true salvation, 51
Security, feelings of, 19, 44, 45
Self
  center of universe, 41
  in God's sight, 43
Separation
  aggravates problems, 38, 46
  anxiety, 39
  growth, 43 ff
  marital problems, 21, 44
  married couples, 42
  problem of, 41

Shakespeare, William, 41
Shipp, Tom, 78
Sin, original, 41
Soldier, best, 29
Stein, Gertrude, 109
Suicide
    potential, 27
Sullivan, Harry Stack, 39

Thurber, James, 39

Verbatim
    in counseling by letter, 54

Wayne, John, 62
Wesley, John, 135
Wolfe, Thomas, 126